Equality and the
Rights of Women

Equality and the
Rights of Women

Elizabeth H. Wolgast

Cornell University Press

ITHACA AND LONDON

First published 1980 by Cornell University Press.
Published in the United Kingdom
by Cornell University Press Ltd.,
2-4 Brook Street, London W1Y 1AA.

International Standard Book Number 0-8014-1211-0
Library of Congress Catalog Card Number 79-24710
Printed in the United States of America
*Librarians: Library of Congress cataloging information
appears on the last page of the book.*

Virginia Honoski Radner

1927–1976

Contents

Acknowledgments

The research and writing of this book depended on a Fellowship from the National Endowment for the Humanities and on the warm encouragement of Gregory Vlastos and Willis Doney, who from the first thought the book should be written.

Many others contributed. Philosophers who gave valuable suggestions include Steven Sapontzis, Gregory Vlastos, Joel Feinberg, Alan Milne, Georgia Binns Bassen, Newton Garver, Peter Winch, and Fred Berger. Political scientists Emily Stoper and Malcom Smith also helped, particularly with the section on law. I am indebted to Richard Wasserstrom for discussions and for twice making his work available to me prior to publication.

Among my other advisers were Eva Peters Hunting, Elsie Myers Stainton, Marianne Leppmann, Louise Gray, Mari Vlastos, Alice Wolff, and Janice Peek. Each helped one way or other to sharpen and deepen my understanding of what is wrong with the place of women in our form of political thinking. To Katherine Lewis I owe special thanks

Acknowledgments

for her affectionate support and the respite of her sunny studio.

The last debt is a large one, owed to my husband, Richard, and my children, Stephen and Johanna, who give their unqualified support to my philosophical work, whatever direction it goes. I am particularly grateful to Johanna for checking the manuscript and footnotes and also for granting, finally, her agreement with what I had to say.

E. H. W.

Berkeley, California

Equality and the
Rights of Women

Introduction

Where there is equality, can there fail to be justice? Can we take for granted that equal treatment will remedy injustice?

Running through our political tradition is the idea that, underneath, people are the same: the wealthy and the poor, the owner of slaves and the slave, a man in authority and a man under it. We are inclined to say that, stripped of the accidents and trappings brought about by chance, these individuals could change places. The slave and slaveowner might, but for accidents of fate, be in each other's shoes. The prince might change places with the pauper. This view of society encourages us to think of any person as having only the essential characteristics, needs, and concerns of all the rest.

But when we substitute "woman" for "slave" and "pauper" in such traditional formulas, the result is implausible. It is not obvious that, accidents and trappings aside, women share the set of their basic interests with men. And if women are irreducibly different in respect to some of these, then to the degree of the difference, the places cannot

13

be changed. The prince who can change places with a pauper may be unable to change places with a princess.

Arguments supporting equal rights for men and women often stress the similarity of their needs and concerns. And if justice means providing equal rights to all, then, by implication, such rights must be appropriate to everyone. But what if the needs and concerns are different?

Among the forces that push us and shape us are the concepts we are accustomed to using. They, like psychological forces and social mores, shape our reasoning, our expectations, and so our form of life. In this way, arguing for women's rights under the banner of equality encourages women to identify their interests with those of men. What is good for men, this reasoning requires, must be good for women too. To bear babies, since it does not pertain also to men, does not figure in the equalitarian's vision. For women to identify themselves as women—therefore different from men—changes the logical basis of the reasoning, and so undermines what appears the best argument they have for their rights. In asserting their difference, it seems, women are courting their own disadvantage.

When we think about justice in terms of equality, a consequence appears that whatever is not an instance of equality seems to be one of *in*equality. And to our ears inequality has the ring of injustice, of unfairness and discrimination. What, we wonder, could possibly justify the claim of human inequality?

At bottom of my argument is the conviction that justice requires men and women to be treated differently, not in all areas but in some important ones. It is not just a curious fact that men never bear babies. Nor do women bear them because society teaches them how and insists they do, while guarding this knowledge from men. And from this difference other consequences flow. A good society will acknowledge the differences, treating them with respect and fairness and accommodating institutions to the human condition. To proceed otherwise is to imitate Procrustes, who invited guests to spend the night and then cut them down or stretched them to fit his bed. It is to be guided by a strange sense of priorities.

In order to formulate suitable programs and to argue for the rights women need, appropriate concepts are essential. And equality will not be first among them; in many respects it is unsuitable, inappropriate, misleading. As Mary Midgley observed, trying to right the injustices that women bear, by using the concepts of equality and freedom "is like trying to dig a garden with a brush and comb. The tools are totally unsuitable."[1]

I will approach the subject of women's rights by looking at how and where egalitarian arguments lead and then ask: Is this a logical route to the various rights women need? Is this the way we want to go? If not, then it is self-defeating to hold to an egalitarian framework.

The plan of argument is this: first to consider the claim to human equality based on similarity, and show that while it works for race it fails for sex; then to consider two interpretations of equality, one applying to the most mundane things, the other particularly to social situations, and ask what it would mean in each to say that humans are equal. In neither case is it plausible to say so. Then, turning to Supreme Court cases the question is put: How has equality worked to settle disputes of law? If we are committed to equality, just what legal applications of the term are we committed to? We find the same difficulties that confront us confronting the Supreme Court. Next comes the question why we are so inclined to view humans as sexless, when one considers the importance of sex differences to most species. The answer has to do with our view of human nature as spiritual and rational, our disdain for what counts as animal or merely physical about us. Last is a brief examination of the idea that society is a collection of individuals, as autonomous and separate as molecules of gas in a container. Here is an atomistic view, one that gives credence to the individualistic values of equality and freedom, and to fair competition as a just principle for society. The question is whether or not this is a good model for an enlightened humanity.

It is my thesis that a profound difficulty for the advance of women's rights is conceptual. We need an alternative to egalitarian reasoning. One such alternative would be a bivalent form of thinking, a form that distinguishes between the interests of men and the interests of women. Women, it could be argued, need to represent their own concerns and should not expect them to be represented by men. This is clearest in matters of family and maternity care, but a case could also be made in regard to the economic dependence of women, their opportunities for employment, and provisions for their later years. Such a bivalent view provides a justification for affirmative action policies because it rejects a neutral perspective from which the concerns of both sexes can be seen "objectively." It supports the idea that women contribute distinctively to their professions and fields of interest, to the diversity of our culture and the richness of its values. And it casts suspicion on the idea that women's qualifications for various endeavors should be judged exclusively by men.

But I do not think this bivalent view can give the full solution to the problems raised by the atomistic-egalitarian model. For an adequate solution, it would be necessary to replace this model by one that gives emphasis to human connections, to forms of human interdependence, and to the needs that lead to them. Many important facts should be taken into account: that a baby needs someone's time-consuming love and care; that elderly persons are unable to compete for their sustenance; that childbearing and child-nurturing are not primarily ways to satisfy self-oriented desires; that families are not associations of individuals who join together for their mutual benefit. A model that cannot reasonably represent these facts is just not an acceptable model of human society.

If men and women have somewhat different perspectives and concerns, as I argue, then it seems reasonable that a new model of society would profit from contributions by women, even though some of these contributions may be ajar with tradition. In that cause, truly, this work has been written.

CHAPTER ONE Equality of the Sexes

Equality is the key to arguments for many kinds of rights and against many kinds of injustices—against slavery, despotism, economic exlpoitation, the subjection of women, racial oppression. It is not surprising then that arguments for women's rights turn on the notion of equality. But it is wonderful that one idea can serve so many causes. Does it always work the same, for instance, in regard to race and sex? And particularly, what does equality mean when applied to men and women?

I

If people were all alike there would be no question about their equality. Thus the claim of human equality is often linked with the assertion of human similarity. The philosopher John Locke, for instance, said that there is "nothing more evident than that creatures of the same species and rank, promiscuously born to all the same advantages of nature and the use of the same facultics, should also be equal one amongst another without subordination or subjection."[1]

Insofar as they are similar in birth and faculties they should be equal in society.

From the equality of men it is natural to infer the equality of their principal rights. "Equals must be equal in rights," one scholar expressed it.[2] If men are equal, then none is privileged by nature, and their rights, like the men themselves, should be similar.

These ways of reasoning are very familiar in discussions of racial equality. Differences of race such as skin color and hair texture are superficial, it is argued; in the important respects the races are similar and therefore equal. To distinguish between the rights of one group and the rights of another when the only differences are these unimportant ones seems patently unjust. So an argument for racial equality based on similarity is tantamount to an argument for equal rights regardless of race.

Women's rights are commonly argued on the same lines. The first step is the assertion of their similarity with men, and the last step is the claim that they should have equal rights. The nineteenth-century philosopher John Stuart Mill argued in this way, long before most philosophers addressed the problem. "There is no natural inequality between the sexes," he claimed, "except perhaps in bodily strength." Women can be thought of as weak men. Now strength by itself is not a good ground for distinguishing among people's rights. Mill infers, "If nature has not made men and women unequal, still less ought the law to make them so." As in the case of race, similarity dictates similar treatment. "Men and women ought to be perfectly co-equal," and "a woman ought not to be dependent on a man, more than a man on a woman, except so far as their affections make them so."[3]

If women are like men except perhaps for strength, the argument for sexual equality would be even more powerful than that for racial equality; for with race the differences are several and determined by heredity, while women and men may have the same genetic components and transmit the same ones. If strength alone differentiated women from men, sex equality would be perfectly apparent.

But of course women are not weak men, and Mill is not deceived. Women are talented like men and have imagination, determination, drive, and other capacities the same as men; but they are different in ways other than strength. Sometimes Mill acknowledges differences, even stresses their importance. He thinks that, while a woman should be able to support herself, "in the natural course of events she will *not*," but her husband will support them both. "It will be for the happiness of both that her occupation should rather be to adorn and beautify" their lives.[4] At the same time her commitment to the home is a large one.

> Like a man when he chooses a profession, so, when a woman marries, it may in general be understood that she makes choice of the management of a household and the bringing up of a family, as the first call upon her exertions, during as many years of her life as may be required for the purpose; and that she renounces . . . all [other occupations] which are not consistent with the requirements of this.[5]

Women should conform to an inflexible set of demands by household and family. Their role does not stem from their weakness—that wouldn't make sense. The real reason for women having this role is that they are the "opposite" sex and the ones to have children. That "coequality" Mill advocates turns out to be a "natural arrangement" with man and wife "each being absolute in the executive branch of their own department."[6] What happened to the equality nature provided? It was not so clear after all.

Mill is more convincing when he speaks of the particular

virtues in which the sexes differ. Women have their distinctive contribution to make, he says: they bring depth to issues where men bring breadth; they are practical where men are theoretical; they introduce sentiment where it is needed and would otherwise be lacking; and of course women are especially apt in the care and training of children.[7] To extol these characteristics of women, Mill must put aside that similarity which first supported equality of rights; but here his respect for women is unequivocal and plain.

In sum, Mill is ambivalent about the similarity of the sexes. On the one hand he argues as if women were weak men, on the other, that they have their distinctive and important virtues. On the one hand he espouses legal equality; on the other he endorses a conventional dependent role for married women.

If Mill's claim for sexual equality rested entirely on similarity, it would seem that that equality is in jeopardy. But he has another defense ready. There is, he says, "an *a priori* assumption . . . in favour of freedom and impartiality . . . [and] the law should be no respecter of persons, but should treat all alike, save where dissimilarity of treatment is required by positive reasons."[8] Similar treatment is right by presumption, and dissimilar treatment will always need positive justification. The argument from similarity was unnecessary then. But what kind of reason would justify differences of treatment? Mill doesn't say.

An argument for sex equality deriving from similarity is one that stresses the ways in which men and women are alike. But of course they are not exactly alike or there would not be a problem in the first place. It becomes necessary to make some such statement as: they are alike in all *important* respects, just as people of different races are importantly alike and only trivially different. But now it is necessary to consider whether differences of sex really are trivial.

In the case of race it seems clear that skin color and hair and features are unimportant, being superficial. They are mere physical marks. Can one say the same about the differences of sex? That is not so clear.

There is also a danger in using the argument from similarity, namely that, while it is meant to justify treating people alike, it implies that if people were importantly different they might need to be treated differently. So by implication it allows differences between individuals to justify *un*equal rights. This feature shows the importance for this kind of reasoning of maintaining that differences of sex are really trivial, for if they are not shown to be so, the argument can work against equality of rights.

Consider this argument: Sex, like skin color and other features of race, is a merely biological characteristic. It is an aspect of a person's physical composition like the chemical constituents of cells, and has nothing to do with the person as a moral entity. The sex of a person, like these other characteristics, should have no influence on how she or he is treated. I call this the "mere biology" argument.

It is true that skin color is an unimportant difference and should not affect a person's rights. But it is not unimportant *for the reason that it is biological.* The difference between men and apes is merely biological too, as is the difference between men and fishes; yet these differences rightly lead to different treatment. Who says we must treat all biological forms alike? Indeed, among humans some biological differences justify differences of treatment, as helping a blind person and caring for a baby clearly show. The "mere biology" argument is therefore a bad one.

How can it be argued that sex is an unimportant difference? We can see the issue more clearly through a form of sex egalitarianism more sophisticated and modern than Mill's. Richard Wasserstrom, a philosopher and lawyer, argues that the good society would give no more recognition to sex or racial differences than we presently give to eye color. "Eye color is an irrelevant category" he argues, "nobody cares what color people's eyes are; it is not an important cultural fact; nothing turns on what eye color you have."[9] No laws or institutions distinguish between persons by eye color, nor do even personal decisions turn on it. The same would hold, in the good society, of racial and sexual differences. The good society would be "assimilationist" with respect to race and sex just as our society is with respect to eye color.

Race and sex and eye color would all be viewed in the same way if our society were just. All three kinds of difference are biological, natural; but among them sex is "deeper," he concedes, and seems to have greater social implications:

> What opponents of assimilationism seize upon is that sexual difference appears to be a naturally occurring category of obvious and inevitable social relevance in a way, or to a degree, which race is not.... An analysis of the social realities reveals that it is the socially created sexual differences which tend in fact to matter the most. It is sex-role differentiation, not gender per se, that makes men and women as different as they are from each other.[10]

It is the way we recognize sex differences in socially created sex roles that gives them their great importance. If we stopped such artificial forms of recognition, we would see that the underlying difference of sex, like that of race, is trivial. Even though it is a naturally occurring difference, that in itself does not justify a social distinction, a distinction in roles. The principle difference of sex is social, not biological. And so sex is analogous to race: the difference allows for assimilation, given a change in laws, in institutions, and in social mores. Although there will still *be* a sexual difference, it will not make a difference.

To compare sex and race in this way implies that reproductive differences and reproduction itself should not much affect our social arrangements: "There appear to be very few, if any, respects in which the ineradicable, naturally occurring differences between males and females *must* be taken into account," Wasserstrom says.[11] The differences can just be ignored. But how do we ignore the reproductive differences? They are not many or very important, he argues, given the present state of medical knowledge:

> Sexual intercourse is not necessary, for artificial insemination is available. Neither marriage nor the family is required for conception or child rearing. Given the present state of medical knowledge and the natural realities of female pregnancy, it is difficult to see why any important institutional or interpersonal arrangements must take the existing gender difference of *in utero* pregnancy into account.[12]

When you consider how many differences can be compensated for by medical innovations, there is only the nine months of *in utero* pregnancy left. And why should that make very much difference? Wasserstrom thinks it shouldn't. The sexes should be treated the same. Here is a variation of the "mere biology" argument, a "mere pregnancy" argument.

In the good society there is sex equality: that is a primary consideration. For treating similar people the same would seem inherently just. If therefore it is within our means to make people more similar, through science and medicine, that course has much to recommend it; for with equality the goodness of society is assured. "Even though there are biological differences between men and women by nature, this fact does not determine the question of what the good society can and should make of these differences," Wasserstrom writes.[13] We don't need to be guided by nature; we can use our intelligence to control, adjust, and compensate for the differences nature produces.

Wasserstrom is not, like Mill, guided by existing similarities but is committed to create similarities wherever possible. Equality of the sexes is an ideal, an ideal of justice, and it requires similarities to exist. The good society, then, will create the similarities to go with its ideal, and that means it will create conditions under which its citizens will be, in all important ways, sexually similar.

I will not stop to consider whether this ideal is a pleasant or attractive one, for I want to ask the question: Is it true that merely biological differences of sex should not influence a good society?

II

Part of the egalitarian view expressed most commonly is the idea that biological differences of sex can be separated from social roles. Then the question is raised whether different sex roles, which are social artifacts, are desirable. Put this way, it is difficult to see why the roles should be very different. But it is not clear that the biological differences and the social ones *are* so distinct and separate.

Take the one fact, mentioned by Wasserstrom as unalterable at present, that women bear children after a period of pregnancy. From this one fact of *in utero* pregnancy one consequence directly follows: a woman does not normally have occasion to wonder whether the baby she bears is hers. She does not wonder if she or someone else is the mother. The father stands in a different relation to his child at the outset; his position is logically more distant, depending on inferences a mother need not make. And it is possible that he may doubt and, doubting, even fail to acknowledge a child that is in fact his, while it is difficult to imagine a mother in just that position—to imagine her bearing a child and then wondering whose it can be.

It is easy to imagine confusion about babies in the context of a modern hospital nursery, of course, but what I call attention to is a deeper and inherent asymmetry in parenthood, one that does not stem from institutions but from reproduction itself. As parents mothers have a primary place, one that cannot be occupied by a father.

This fact in turn has consequences. From the fact that mothers are primary parents it is clear that in general a mother is the more easily identifiable of a child's parents. This is important because a child is a very dependent creature and dependent for a very long time. Someone must have responsibility for it, and most generally that responsibility is given to parents. So now, in assigning responsibility for a child, it is simpler and less equivocal to assign the responsibility to a mother than to a father. This is so because doubts can be raised about his parenthood that have no analogue for hers.

From the mere fact of the way children are born, then, there are consequences important to society. Society, in its need to recognize someone as responsible for a child, rightly makes use of this fact of reproduction, the *in utero* pregnancy, so it can identify one parent with reasonable certainty.

I am assuming that parents are responsible for their children. However, this need not be part of the morality of a society, though it is part of the morality of most, and certainly part of ours. If this assumption is not made, the consequences would be different, depending on how society construes the relation of parent and child and places responsibility for the young. But it seems plausible that there will be some connection between parenthood and responsibility, and this connection will reflect the fact that mothers are primary parents.

That mothers are primary parents affects not only laws and institutions but also the way women look at their lives. The potential of pregnancy and motherhood are present from the time girls reach adolescence, and are part of a young female's life and thought in a way they cannot be for a male. She needs to consider parenthood's connection with her behavior, and this influences her options. It would be surprising if it did not also affect her relations with males, sharpening her sense of their polarity, arousing concern about the durability and stability of her relationships with them. In such ways the merely biological fact of *in utero* pregnancy comes to give different coloring to the sexual identity of males and females, laying the groundwork for some sex roles.

Nor is this all. In a society where paternal responsibility is recognized and valued, there is a need to identify males as fathers. Thus an institution that makes formal identification of fathers, such as marriage, becomes important. As a child has two biological parents, so it comes to have two parents in society, within a social structure. And it would be surprising if some mores involving chastity and fidelity did not arise as well. In this way the merely biological facts of reproduction will tend to influence both the form of society and its customs, even though the details of that influence will vary. Societies are not all formed alike; other influences are at work as well. My point is that the fact of *in utero* pregnancy will have some consequences connected with the asymmetry of parenthood. Wasserstrom complains that society "mistakenly leads many persons to the view that women are both naturally and necessarily better suited than men to be assigned the primary responsibilities of child rearing."[14] If he had said "better situated," the observation he attributes to society would be profoundly right. The maternal role *is* more closely connected to parental responsibility than the paternal one, and neither talents nor conditioning nor tastes enter into it.

Suppose a society chooses not to acknowledge the asymmetry of parenthood. How would it do this? Would it assign equal responsibility to both parents? But what about the cases in which the father of an infant is unknown? It has a father, unless he is since deceased; but knowing this is no help. And what of the cases in which a mother refuses to acknowledge any father; is the child not then exclusively hers? In Hawthorne's *The Scarlet Letter*, Hester Prynne's Pearl is *hers*, although both she and the Reverend Dimmesdale know he is the father. How would the good society make that parenting equal?

I do not mean at all that fathers are less tender, less devoted, or less responsible than mothers, that parental solicitude and devotion are women's prerogatives. *That* kind of "sex role" is not implied by the primary parenthood of mothers. What is meant is that asymmetries of parenthood are neither small nor trivial. And because of this they will have asymmetrical effects on other aspects of a person's life, some only indirectly related to parenthood. In this sense of "sex role," it is difficult to understand how sex roles could be abolished or made alike. Would one have to ignore the asymmetries of reproduction? But that would be a pretense.

Since the parental roles are asymmetrical, a natural consequence is some asymmetry in the attitudes of young men and young women regarding both reproduction and sex. The same behavior, sexual intercourse for instance, will have different significance for each. A society that gives structure to these differences, that provides a context into which both genders are expected to fit, will thereby provide for differences in sex roles. A great deal may be embroidered here in the way of stereotypes, rituals, myths, and mores. But what I shall mean by sex roles is a minimal set of differences, differences in attitude and behavior and in life outlook, stemming from the asymmetries of reproduction and framed by a social context.

The answer to Wasserstrom then evolves: The biological differences of men and women do not determine what a good society should make of them, but a good society should take them into account, and probably must do so. In order to justify ignoring the asymmetries that characterize human reproduction, that form of reproduction would have to be drastically changed.

So long as babies develop *in utero* and not, for example, in bottles, parenthood will be an asymmetrical business. A good society will no more ignore it than it will ignore the fact that humans start out as babies and do not live forever.

Wasserstrom's next step may be the proposal that reproduction be changed so as to be more symmetrical, for example, by developing fetuses in the laboratory and delivering them at term to two symmetrically related parents. In this situation a child would have no primary parent; on both sides recognition of parenthood would depend on a similar inference. It is difficult to see that from either the child's point of view or society's this loss of a primary parent would be an improvement.

Sex equality does not always take such a radical form as Wasserstrom gives it. The feminist philosopher Alison Jaggar, for instance, adopts a more moderate position:

A sexually egalitarian society is one in which virtually no public recognition is given to the fact that there is a physiological sex difference between persons. This is not to say that the different reproductive function of each sex should be unacknowledged in such a society nor that there should be no physicians specializing in female and male complaints, etc. But it is to say that, except in this sort of context, the question whether someone is female or male should have no significance.[15]

There will be "virtually" no public recognition of physiological sex differences—this is difficult to understand in concrete terms. There will be medical specialists in male and female complaints; there will presumably be maternity facilities; there will presumably be some provisions for infants of unwed mothers. Are not these all forms of "public recognition"? And don't they work asymmetrically with regard to the sexes? Perhaps Jaggar means to exclude issues connected with parenthood from her general rule, so that these asymmetries can be publicly recognized. Such things as maternity leaves and child support for unwed mothers would then qualify for public recognition. What would not qualify would be matters in respect to which women and men *should not* be treated differently in the first place. If this is the gist of her view, then it is substantially like mine. The question is why it should be called "egalitarian."

In Wasserstrom's ideal, people will regard one another, even in personal matters, without distinguishing the sexes. We don't distinguish between people on the basis of eye color: "so the normal, typical adult in this kind of nonsexist society would be indifferent to the sexual, physiological differences of other persons for all interpersonal relationships. Bisexuality, not heterosexuality or homosexuality, would be the norm."[16] In order for the sexes to be really equal, he reasons, we need to treat them alike even in personal and private ways. For if there are sex distinctions regularly made in private, they will be echoed somehow in the public sphere, and this means there will be a sex-differentiated form of society. This cure for sexual injustice is extreme: what is required here is a society of individuals who behave and are treated as if they were sexually alike. It requires an androgynous society.

III

Sex equality based on the similarity of the sexes, as advocated by Wasserstrom, will lead to an assimilationist form of society, for insofar as people are similar, similar treatment of them will be justified, and the assimilationist society treats everyone alike. It ignores sex differences just as it ignores racial ones, and for the same reason—because they are unimportant. By this reasoning a nonassimilationist form of society will necessarily be unjust. Wasserstrom writes:

> Any... nonassimilationist society will make one's sexual identity an important characteristic, so that there are substantial psychological, role, and status differences between persons who are males and those who are females.... [But] sex roles, and all that accompany them, necessarily impose limits—restrictions on what one can do, be or become. As such, they are, I think, at least prima facie wrong.[17]

In restricting us sex roles are wrong. Through them "involuntarily assumed restraints have been imposed on the most central factors concerning the way one will shape and live one's life."[18] But sex roles in the narrow sense I mean them are reflections of restrictions; they do not create restrictions or impose them. Rather the restrictions come from the way human reproduction works and the kinds of responsibilities it entails in the framework of a real human society. It is hard to speak of the restrictions being imposed, just as it is hard to think of the character of human vision imposing restrictions on us. We cannot see what is behind our heads at any given moment; that is frustrating and certainly limits our freedom, restricting what we can do, be, or become. But one wouldn't for that reason call the visual system "wrong." Living in a society involves restrictions too, and so does being born to particular parents, in a particular place, in this century. These things too affect "the most central factors concerning the way one will shape and live one's life." But from what point of view can we term them "wrong"? We do not have an abstract viewpoint from which to measure the "wrongness" of such accidents.

Our difficulty with the assimilationist ideal has two sides: On the one, it seems to be based on human similarity, on the triviality of sex differences. But, as I argue, there is much reason to reject this and much justification for recognizing some form of sex roles. On the other hand, the assimilationist ideal seems to commit one to *creating* similarities, through medical and social measures, as if the ideal did not rest on anything, but were self-evident. If all sex roles are wrong, then only a unisex form of society will be just. But we are not unisex creatures; we are not androgynous or hermaphroditic. So assimilationism seems an inappropriate ideal, at least for human beings.

Having sex roles is natural to us and not the creation of society. As Midgley says, maternal instinct is not reducible to "cultural conditioning by the women's magazines."[19] If equality were adopted as an ideal, a massive effort at conditioning would be necessary to make us think like androgynous creatures with similar sex roles and sexual natures and so to fit that form of society. It is the androgynous role that is artificial, the product of a fictitious view of human nature. Instead of encouraging freedom and autonomy, the assimilationist society would thus restrict us to an androgynous form of life. It is a kind of Procrustean bed.

IV

Sex is a deeper phenomenon than race, Wasserstrom concedes. Its differences are more pervasive, more securely built into our institutions and practices. Nevertheless, he believes sex can be treated along the same lines as race, without qualitative adjustments. Lumping race and sex together is also common where there is talk of "group discrimination" and programs to combat it. But the cases are not alike.

One way to see the difference is to consider the way "assimilation" applies in the two cases. It is conceivable that, with less strictness in our mores, the races would come eventually to be assimilated to one. Differences in color and physiognomy would be so muted as to count only as individual ones, on a par with eye color. There is the possibility of real, genetic assimilation in the case of race. But with sex this is obviously not possible, and even if it were, we would have to think hard whether we wanted it. To allow equality to determine the character of our species seems to show a wrong order of things.

Equality based on similarity is connected to the Aristotelian dictum that we should treat likes alike and unlikes differently. But which cases are alike and which different? The answer is not simple. In the matter of race we generally say the cases are alike; in the case of sex this is not at all obvious. The difference of sex is genetically nonassimilable and besides it is difficult to ignore. Perhaps Aristotle's rule should lead us to conclude that with sex the cases require different treatment.

Where similarity is a consideration, racial arguments and sexual ones need to be separated. A person's racial characteristics are not usually correlated with special concerns differentiating racial groups, while many of women's most important concerns, for instance those connected with pregnancy, are distinctive to women as a group. The fair treatment of the two sexes cannot be assumed to consist in the "assimilation" of their rights.

Less compelling is the fact that sex differences have a lot to do with our enjoyment of human relationships. *Could* we treat the sexes alike as Wasserstrom proposes? We normally respond differently to members of the opposite sex than to members of our own. Even putting sexual attraction aside, we still have different relations to members of different sexes. With members of our sex, we have and anticipate having, a good deal in common. To a child we say, "When I was a little girl . . ." (if we are women) with the implication that we lack the same identification with boys. While with members of the opposite sex we perceive contrasts and divergent points of view, for some areas of common experience are lacking. Understanding those other persepectives is often a tenuous matter, ignorance and mystery being the conditions it must work against; but it is also one that fascinates, challenges, delights, and amuses us.

Wasserstrom could respond that these differences are mostly the creation of society, and that the position I suggest amounts to an endorsement of present sex roles and stereotypes. This is not intended. What I propose is rather that biology differentiates us in ways that will have some implications for differentiated sex roles. It is not a "solution" to such differentiation to suggest that everyone have the same roles or pretend to have them. The feminist social critic Dorothy Dinnerstein argues in *The Mermaid and the Minotaur* that "gender symbiosis" is a neurotic condition that needs correcting.[20] Although I agree with many of her observations about sex roles in our society and the need for changes, I am arguing that asymmetry will persist in some form or other, that the implications of biology are pervasive. The idea that, under propitious conditions, sex differences can be flattened out or "nullified" does not seem either necessary or attractive.[21] Nor is it clearly possible. It may be no more possible for us to treat people of different sexes alike than it is for us to treat a baby as an adult, or an elderly man as a youth. Some differences cannot be discounted.

v

Our commitment to equality is deep. It goes back at least to Aristotle, who, though he was not egalitarian in our sense, defined justice as "a kind of equality."[22] The problem is how to translate this. On one side the philosopher Hugo Bedau insists that all forms of equality "involve sameness, in the same sense of 'same.' That is why they are equalities."[23] On the other side David Thomson claims that "the idea of equality has nothing to do with uniformity. To recognize that men are all equally individual human beings involves no desire or need to treat them uniformly in any ways other than those in which they clearly have a moral claim to be treated alike."[24] Equality can be detached from similarity, according to this, and from equal treatment as well.

A parallel dispute arises about rights and whether they should be equal. One egalitarian philosopher, Gregory Vlastos, argues that they neither are nor should be:

> The holder of a unique political office . . . would not be equal in all rights to all other men or even to one other man: no other man would have equal right to this office, or to as high an office. . . . Why don't [the authors of egalitarian documents] come out and say that men are born and remain equal in some rights, but are either not born or do not remain equal in a great many others?[25]

He asks pointedly, "Would anyone wish to say that there are no just inequalities?" Moreover, to treat anything that is just as some form of equality is illogical, as Bedau observes:

> Philosophers have assumed, or come close to assuming, that because an inequality may be just or justified, it is really an equality after all, as though the justice or justifiability of certain arrangements could only be expressed by pronouncing the arrangement "equal," as though the most important thing to say on the behalf of the morality of an arrangement is that it is equal.[26]

The debate is very confusing. Differences among women and men seem to be relevant to their equality and the equality of their rights; and it seems, as the philosopher Isaiah Berlin says, that "so long as there are differences

between men, some degree of inequality may occur."[27]
Even while committed to equality, we resist being committed to sameness. We do not want to rest all arguments for equal rights on similarity, any more than Lincoln did in this argument against Douglas:

> Certainly the negro is not our equal in color—perhaps not in many other respects; still, in the right to put into his mouth the bread that his own hands have earned, he is the equal of every other man, white or black. In pointing out that more has been given you, you can not be justified in taking away the little which has been given him. All I ask for the negro is that if you do not like him, let him alone. If God gave him but little, that little let him enjoy.[28]

Here the appeals to racial equality and similarity are dropped; the Negro has equal rights independent of these.

A great advantage of the assimilationist ideal is its simplicity. Within it we can easily say whether rights are distributed justly or not, for we need only see whether they are equal. But, as Wasserstrom concedes, simplicity cannot be its chief justification.[29] And as similarity has been found unsatisfactory as a ground for equality and as a guide to interpreting it, we turn to examine equality in two other meanings. The first I term "strict" equality; the second is the equality of peers.

CHAPTER TWO

Things Being Equal

Equality is a term of ordinary and practical use, not distinctively a philosophical one. If we look at how it applies to things in ordinary contexts, that may shed light on its importance in social ones. Let us ask what, in a mundane sense, it would mean to say that humans are equal.

I

If two things are unequal, one is greater and the other less. If two planks are unequal, one is larger and the other smaller. And the same with two pieces of cake; they are unequal when one is larger than the other.

To be unequal, things must be different in some way, but being different is not enough by itself. A dog and a cat are different, but not unequal. A rose and a hyacinth are different, but not unequal. In these cases we do not think of the one thing as being greater than the other. They are merely different.

Besides being different, unequal things must differ in some respect like a gradation of quality. They need to differ in a feature that is subject to comparison. Otherwise "greater" and "less" do not make sense. You wouldn't be understood if you said that a rose and a hyacinth were unequal, not unless it was understood what standard of comparison you had in mind. There might be such a measure—depth of color, for instance, or size, or even fragrance. But the judgment of inequality and a measure go together, the former requires the latter.

Measures may be disputed. Two art critics may argue about *what* difference makes a work of art better than another. But a judgment of inequality presumes that there is *some* measure, otherwise the judgment would not make sense.

Now look at the opposite of inequality—equality. If two things are equal, this means they are not unequal; one is not greater and the other less. Whatever the measure, both things satisfy it, both measure the same. So if two planks are equal, their length is the same. They might have been unequal but they aren't. So, like a judgment of inequality, one of equality also implies that there is a measure according to which the one thing *might be* greater than the other. Put another way the equality of two things presupposes the possibility of their inequality, for that's what a measure signifies. In this way the concept of equality sits on the possibility of inequality, and without it would not make sense.

As a dog and a cat are not unequal, they are not equal either. And a rose and a hyacinth are neither equal nor unequal. Neither "equality" nor "inequality" apply, because in these instances a measure is lacking.

Now consider the way judgments of human equality are normally supposed to work. If two people are not equal we infer that they must be unequal. We suppose that the denial of inequality must be the same as an assertion of equality, that there is no third alternative. We seem to suppose that equality or inequality, being simple alternatives, will characterize any pair of things. (Of course we don't *really* *think* that any pair of things will be equal or unequal, a rainbow and a Wordsworth ode for instance. But we lightly adopt sweeping generalizations about terms like these, without really thinking much at all. Of such stuff are philosophical problems often composed.) But if equality works as we have described, such inferences are wrong. To say that two things are not unequal need not mean that they are equal. They may just be different, unrelated by a measure. And this is clearly the case with many pairs of things we can think of: we have no measure or standard for comparing them. We can't consider any two things and ask, which is greater? A cow and a windmill, a hammer and screwdriver, a loaf of bread and a pudding. The absence of a measure does not simply stem from things being of different sorts. Even for very similar things there may be no measure for judging their inequality. The queen in *Snow White* might have heard her mirror say that there is no measure by which all beautiful persons can be ranked, no "fairest of all."

Taking any pair of things at random, we have no guarantee that there is an answer to the question, are they equal or not? Even among roses some excel in one way, others in another. And when the standard *is* specified, differences may still make it difficult to say which is greater, as a judge can find at a flower show. Judgments of equality and inequality are often difficult and imprecise.

Now let us use this analysis of judgments of equality and inequality to try to understand the equality of men.

II

Suppose you went to the lumberyard looking for a plank to use for a job of repairing. As you look at a stack of planks, seeing only the ends, you would be interested to hear that they are all equal, that they measure the same. What is important about knowing this? What difference does it make? This: from the remark that they are equal it follows that one plank is substitutable for any other. You can choose one randomly and without regard for individual differences, without discrimination; you can do this *because* they are all equal.

Planks may be unequal in color or clarity even while they are equal in length, so it is sometimes necessary to specify that respect in which they are being compared. But to say things are *simply equal* will normally imply that for ordinary and understood purposes one can be freely substituted for another. Differences among them will not matter.

Saying that all men are equal should, by analogy, imply that men are substitutable for one another. What can this mean? Not that they are equally useful for some purpose. But it may be understood to mean, for example, that no one's vote is to count any more than any other's; with respect to their votes they all count the same; they are equal, substitutable. Individual differences do not matter. In the same way people are substitutable when it comes to jury duty. They are not picked according to their individual characteristics but randomly, which is to say, without concern for *which* person exactly is chosen. And in commercial dealings, each person expects to be treated the same as any other without concern for features or identity. With regard to these matters all men are supposed to be the same. To distinguish treatment of them according to their differences would be discriminatory and unfair.

That people are substitutable for one another is therefore a consequence of the proposition that they are equal, just as the substitutability of planks follows from their equality. Equality of men gives a premise, then, for the claim that people ought to be treated exactly the same in some respect or other, that they have equal rights. And the sense of "equal rights" is captured by the notion of substitutability.

If men are equal, their rights should be the same, we tend to reason. To object to equal rights for Negroes implies that there is some sense in which they are not the equals of others. But how can this be justified? Occasionally a writer asserts the inequality of men, simply and without qualification, as does Robert Ardrey (whose view is discussed in Chapter 3). But for most of us this has a morally offensive ring. Since the equality of humans is hard to deny, it has great power to support equality of rights.

Equal rights, rights that entirely neglect individual differences and treat one person as substitutable for any other, form an important part of our political rights. The rights to vote, to be included in jury rolls, to engage in commerce and own property, to be subject to standard rules of law when charged with an offense, to speak one's mind and worship as one wants—all these rights belong to a person regardless of his individual characteristics. Talent, wealth, character, diligence, birthright—none of these is relevant to such rights, however important the characteristics are otherwise. With regard to these rights, humans might as well all be the same.

Isaiah Berlin says that the formula "Every man to count for one and no one to count for more than one" seems to him "to form the heart of the doctrine of equality or of equal rights."[1] This captures some of the notion of substitutability; and the English historian J. R. Pole uses "interchangeability" of individuals in much the same way as I use "substitutability."[2] These are all ways of connecting equal rights with the idea of human equality.

However, equal rights are not the only important ones. Some rights depend on individual differences, on accidents of fortune, on talents, or on other features that distinguish people. These rights are special or differential ones; among them are the right of a blind person to use of a white cane, the right of a veteran to burial at public expense, the right of an indigent to government assistance, the right of a fatherless child to public support. Many rights are of this kind. They are not rights for everyone but rights only for those who qualify, and most of them have a presumptive basis in needs. (This sense of special rights differs from one described by the philosopher H. L. A. Hart, which depends on the relations between people, as for example when one of them has made the other a promise.[3] My sense of special rights relates to groups having some particular characteristics, not to persons standing in a particular relationship.)

The two kinds of rights, equal and differential (or special), work very differently. With regard to an equal right, taking a person's individual qualities into account may constitute discrimination. But with special rights, they *must* be taken into account, for these rights are based on human differences.

Equal rights can be understood as a consequence of a principle of human equality. But the question arises about special rights, whether their justification is consistent with such a principle. If some rights should be unequal, contingent upon human differences, does this imply that men are unequal? How, in short, can the two kinds of rights be reconciled if equal rights depend on a principle of equality?

III

The implications of human differences make egalitarianism difficult to hold. Isaiah Berlin observed that "there is no kind of inequality against which, in principle, a pure egalitarian may not be moved to protest, simply on the ground that he sees no reason for tolerating it." True equality is safe only where there is uniformity: "In its simplest form the ideal of complete social equality embodies the wish that everything and everybody should be as similar as possible to everything and everybody else."[4] Otherwise there would be ground for distinguishing rights. As similarity provided the grounds for equal rights, dissimilarity gives grounds for differential rights. A perfectly egalitarian society needs to prevent differences from appearing or to squelch them, an idea that Kurt Vonnegut exploits in his story "Harrison Bergeron."[5] If one believes that "social inequalities are unnecessary, and unjustifiable, and ought to be eliminated," then the conclusion follows that people ought to be, in any respects that might affect their place in society, the same.[6] Differences among them threaten the equality of their rights.

Aristotle, though he thought justice was a kind of equality, did not mean that people should be treated alike. Only people who are similar should be treated the same; those who are unlike should be treated differently. That seemed only sensible to him. You would not treat a thief like an honest man nor a child like an adult. Plato too was offended by the idea that rights of citizens should be equal and observed that democracy distributes an odd sort of equality, to equals and unequals alike.[7] Our egalitarian way of thinking was not at all obvious to these philosophers.

The distinction between equal rights and special ones requires us to reconcile their justifications, since the equality of men which supports the former seems to conflict with the latter. Do we need two independent kinds of justification? Gregory Vlastos objects: "If we are to have two sets of 'just making' reasons, one set requiring us to uphold [equal or natural] rights, the other permitting us to overrule them, we shall be in a state of moral uncertainty and anxiety about our natural rights." Having two sets of reasons will lead straight to confusion and perplexity about which rights are justified. Moral reasoning is secure only if it is simple. This was one consideration that led to the notion of an assimilationist society; and it leads Vlastos to offer a principle that both supports natural rights and provides "the only moral reasons for just exceptions to them."[8]

The fact that we need both kinds of rights creates a dilemma for an egalitarian: it appears he cannot justify the one kind without undercutting the justification of the other. He would like to say that people are equal in some respects but unequal in others, but this equivocates on the question, are they equal or not?

If equal rights depend on the principle of human equality, this dilemma has no solution. We can't have it both ways: either people are equal and therefore their rights should be the same, or they are not equal and their rights may need to be different. We must at this point reexamine the principle of equality and its role in moral reasoning.

IV

To say that planks are equal implies that there is a measure according to which they all are the same. By analogy, saying that men are equal implies that there is a measure which all of them satisfy. What measure is it? If we take an ordinary natural quality of human beings—age, size, intelligence, for a few—it is evident that, according to these, humans vary widely. The principle of equality requires a characteristic that doesn't vary. What could it be?

A serious problem looms here. For whatever is taken as a measure will allow that men might measure differently even though in fact they don't. That is to say, any measure will make palpable the possibility of human inequality. It gives a definite sense to human inequality, indicating where and when it might exist. Now this implication is offensive to an egalitarian. He does not understand human equality to be a matter of fact, an accident of nature, and means not only that people *are equal* but that they *cannot be unequal*.

However, to exclude the possibility of inequality takes away the sense of equality as well. Under this condition, human equality makes no sense.

If we look at the language of egalitarian thinkers, we find them identifying the character with respect to which all humans are alike in such words as these: men have the same "intrinsic value as individual human beings"; the same value attaches "to the person himself as an integral and unique individual"; people are alike as descendants of Adam and creatures of God.[9] Do these phrases suggest a genuine measure? They do not. On the contrary, as Vlastos says, what is needed for the claim of human equality is not a concept according to which individuals can be graded, for "there is no grading individuals as such." But if there is no grading them, there is no measuring their worth, however it is conceived. That, he would say, is exactly the point.

There is no measure of human beings: *that* is the real egalitarian thesis. There is no measure according to which one human qua human can be said to be greater or less than another. Their worth stands beyond measure. That is what is meant by saying they are equal.

But if this is what is meant by men being equal, the idea is most unfortunately expressed. It is one thing to say that all men are equal, which implies that there is a measure applicable, and quite another to say that men are equal *because no measure of them exists*. For the latter claim to be plausible, it should say that neither equality nor inequality apply to human beings. That says something important about the nature of morality; the other makes us first think of the usefulness of weights and measures and then rejects their connection with equality. It leads to confusion.

Similarly, the language of "worth" and "value" misleads, because these terms are also essentially connected with measures. Saying that all people have equal worth and intrinsic worth is a preface to saying what terms that worth can be expressed in, which means there is some way that the equality of human worth is determined. But none of these implications is meant or wanted. What is meant is that *none of these terms*, strictly taken, applies to humans.

Yet it is not difficult to understand why the egalitarian thesis comes to be expressed as it is. For that thesis is meant to deny that humans are *un*equal, and what clearer way to say this than by saying they are equal? The inference comes naturally that if they are not unequal, they must be equal instead. But this is the step that is wrong. What needs to be understood is that there is no appropriate measure and cannot be one, when the moral status of humans is being considered. According to this truth, neither equality nor inequality among humans is possible. As with a dog and cat, a rose and hyacinth, a hammer and chisel, there are differences, but no differences in the matter of worth.

If we express the egalitarian insight by saying that humans cannot be graded as moral entities, there is no longer a problem about human differences. We can say with Vlastos that moral worth, unlike other kinds of worth, is not gradable.[10] And this is not a trivial thing to say. There are many kinds of value which are measurable and which humans possess—for example, land, wealth, and power—and it is interesting and important to say that none of these is connected with moral respect, to say that all men deserve moral respect alike. It is this profound idea that gets wrongly expressed in the principle of equality.

The importance of the egalitarian view, I propose, is exactly its refusal to allow a measure of human beings. Because of a philosophical confusion, this point does not emerge plainly. If it did, equality as such would not be involved. The egalitarian would not then be concerned to say that people are similar, or be troubled about differences. Neither similarity nor dissimilarity would even appear relevant to the thesis, since it mainly concerns the rejection of measures.

The most persuasive argument for human equality—that men must be equal since they are not unequal—is a bad one. Both alternatives are void unless there are measures for human inequalities, and the stronger moral claim is that there are not.

v

If the principle of equality does not literally mean that humans are equal, then substitutability does not follow from it. But this is not disappointing. We do not want to justify substitutability in general. In many ways people cannot be substituted: no other child is substitutable for your child, nor is one of your children substitutable for another; not just anyone can replace your friend; nor can just anyone replace someone especially trained or talented. If there were a general rule that humans are substitutable, it would not be a good one.

So it is not surprising that not all rights should be equal rights. As Vlastos would say, there are many differences in treatment that are just. The rights of an adult are different from those of a child; the rights of a convicted criminal are different from those of an innocent victim; and blind or handicapped or retarded persons all have special rights because of their differences.

How are such rights justified? Normally they are related to needs that distinguish, and often handicap, a group. A blind person cannot take full advantage of ordinary schooling, or cross a street safely alone, so the rights that pertain especially to him come out of such needs. But they also depend upon technology and customs and institutions. Without the invention of braille the blind could not have a right to materials in braille. Special rights may derive from institutional arrangements as well: for instance, delays in court procedures may work injustices for persons accused of crimes, the remedy for which may be cast in the form of a special right. There is nothing like a "natural" right here; such rights are entirely contingent.

In contrast, many (but not all) equal rights are taken to be more basic. Instead of deriving from institutions, these rights often shape and determine them. Thus the right of citizens to elect their government has a powerful influence on the way government works. And the rights to express our views and worship and associate as we want limit our laws and institutions in various ways.

It might be plausible to distinguish special rights as "benefits" or "privileges" and not rights at all, since they depend upon circumstances and the needs of special groups. Then "rights" could be limited to those general guarantees that pertain to everyone, such as the rights to privacy, free speech, and worship. This way of making the distinction I am concerned with was not chosen because we commonly do speak of "women's rights" and mean to include such benefits as maternity leaves. My terminology simply follows this practice.

It is tempting to try to assimilate these two kinds of rights into one, saying that special rights are rights possessed by everyone in case he or she should ever qualify for them. The right to materials in braille, on this view, is possessed even by those with normal vision, *in the event that they should become blind.* Of course a normal person cannot exercise this right, so it is only potentially his. The idea is at best peculiar. It is strange to say that a person has the rights possessed by someone retarded, to be exercised in the event that he should have been born retarded! Equally absurd is the idea that a man possesses the same rights as a woman, for instance a right to maternity leave or midwifery assistance, which he can exercise in the event he ever becomes female and pregnant. (Interestingly, just this argument is part of a Supreme Court decision, discussed in Chapter 4.)

The principal difference between most equal rights and special ones is that the latter are contingent upon individual characteristics while the former usually are not. The right to have braille materials is possessed only by the blind in virtue of being blind. The right to speak and worship have no such contingent foundation.

One way to characterize the two kinds of rights is to say that, with regard to equal rights, Justice should be blind. No attention should be paid an individual's distinguishing characteristics. While with special rights, qualifications are relevant and important. With regard to these, Justice needs to see, and, to avoid abuses, her vision may need to be sharp. Under this view, differentiating equal and special rights, we can make clearer sense of such phrases as "being born to certain rights" and rights being "inalienable." The words do not mean that a criminal may not be deprived of these rights, but that they do not stem from needs or special conditions. They are presumptive rights. People have these rights anonymously, as faceless members of society. This is the sense captured by the notion of substitutability: with respect to these rights, people are treated as if they were indistinguishable from one another.

It is tempting to speak of the most basic equal rights as having their ground in the moral status of individuals, as if the latter were a kind of premise from which they followed. But it is also correct to say that equal rights help characterize for us what moral status *means*. They are an expression of the respect in which we hold individual humans. Without these rights, to be sure, such status would be diminished.

Nor do the basic equal rights permit the argument that it does not matter whether everyone has them. It was argued by some framers of the Constitution that the right to vote should be restricted to those with special qualifications, since good government depends upon voters who are educated and responsible. And a similar argument was made against granting the vote to Negroes. The opponents of this form of argument did not dispute that there is a connection between educated, responsible voters and good government. The reply to the argument was on a different level, namely that the electorate has a right to decide even for bad government. The universal franchise is not premised upon the probability that the results will be best.[11]

If equal rights are not grounded in an abstract principle, or in a theory of human worth, or in their good consequences, what ground do they have? That men are "born" to certain rights does not say anything about human birth. Instead it says something about those rights, and what it says, I think, is that no qualifications are necessary for their possession. Being born, any person is presumed to qualify. They are "inalienable" not in the sense that we must have them, but in the sense that no argument, particularly not one referring to results, will count against them.

Consider the right to confront your accusers when charged with an offense. What could convince us that this right should be witheld from citizens? The answer is that nothing could. But what justifies it? That is hard to say. Instead of speaking of its justification, we may more naturally say that it embodies the respect in which individuals are held, and helps characterize our conception of just relations between a citizen and his government.

In sum, equal rights are rights with respect to which Justice should be blind, for their possession does not depend upon a person's having any qualifications. On the contrary, these rights require that individual features be put aside and ignored. It should not make any difference whether someone is rich or poor, with or without power, virtuous or sinful, successful or not. Here people are treated alike; to treat them differently is to hazard a charge of discrimination. This is how substitutability works, to emphasize, not a person's individuality, but the need to ignore it.

VI

Equal rights and special rights have very different justifications, the latter depending on facts that may change, on institutions and the existing ways of assisting people with special needs. How are the two kinds of justification related in our arguments about specific rights? It is illuminating to view some of these in retrospect.

The claim that handicapped people have an "equal right" to access to public buildings is sometimes given as the justification for installing wheelchair ramps. Using equal rights in this way implies that handicapped persons are being denied a right, that their right to access is being thwarted and violated. But this way of putting things is misleading. When there are no ramps, the lame and handicapped are not being singled out for discrimination, or sorted out where their distinctive features should be ignored. Just the contrary: their special needs are *not* being remarked. They have an equal right to enter buildings (no one keeps them out); but they are unable to exercise it. What they need is a right to special entrances, allowing them to exercise their equal right of access.

Another case: it is sometimes argued that children with learning handicaps have an "equal right" to education and therefore should have special school facilities. This sounds strange to start with. Such schools relate to special needs; they are schools that normal children might not profit from. We are not discriminating against abnormal children, singling them out for lesser treatment, when we have regular schools. The argument for special education should rather be that there is a specific *need* for it, a gap to be filled if these children are to get some education. The absence of special programs may constitute a kind of injustice but it is not a form of discrimination.

We are reminded in these cases of Bedau's observation that it is popular to characterize any arrangement one approves of as "egalitarian." It is as if an argument for equal rights were regarded as a superior form of argument, to be used even where special rights are wanted and without regard for its appropriateness. Likewise, discrimination, strictly understood, occurs in a context where differential treatment of people is wrong. To charge discrimination, then, is to charge that people are being sorted out when they are not supposed to be—where Justice should be blind. It makes sense only against a background of equal rights.

Straightening out this terminology, while it may clarify our thinking, does not settle any difficult questions about where people may be justly sorted out and where not. For instance, it is considered unfair to sort out applicants for jobs by their sex: men have won the right to be employed as attendants on airliners, to be telephone operators and secretaries; women in their turn have won the right to be telephone linesmen, construction workers, truck drivers, and members of the crew on Navy ships. To exclude applicants from these jobs because of their sex is considered sex discrimination and so inherently unfair: that is the law's position.[12] But nothing forbids sorting people out in a variety of other ways: by geographical location, by intelligence, by attractiveness and personal charm, by congeniality, by family or institutional connection. No law prohibits these ways of screening applicants. So the question arises: Can sorting people out by such means have some of the same results as sex discrimination? While skin color, for example, may be counted a superficial difference, many other characteristics, even some that may be related to race, are not. And when we open these characteristics to question, it is not clear how equality of rights should work.

Minority groups sometimes argue for an "equal right" to positions of status and prominence and training in desirable professions, medicine and law notably. It is argued that the absence of minority members in these professions shows discrimination against the minority groups. But disparate numbers do not prove there is discrimination, for there is no equal right here being violated. There may be unfairness built into the tests or the criteria for admission may be misapplied, but there is no "equal right" of applicants to be admitted to such schools. Here the nature of the wrong is misidentified.

A remedy often sanctioned for correcting an imbalance of racial representation among lawyers and doctors is the institution of racial quotas for the admission of applicants into training for these professions. But quotas raise new questions in the context of equal rights, provoking the charge that they constitute "reverse discrimination," which is to say, a wrong of exactly the same nature as the one they are supposed to correct. The issue is almost hopelessly muddy. As Ronald Dworkin points out in commenting on the Bakke case, admission to medical school has always taken a variety of personal characteristics into account, not only scores and grades.[13] There may have been racial prejudice expressed in making these decisions; but since there is no equal right to admission, even given certain test scores, there is not discrimination when people are denied admission on the basis of their individual characteristics.

One thing that may be needed for fairness is a shift in the criteria used for acceptance. To make race a positive consideration in the selection process is a change in the use of factors, but it is not a change in the nature of the process. I am among those who find the Supreme Court's decision confusing, not least because the social policy that justified affirmative selection programs has no connection with equal rights so far as I can see.[14] Its justification is of a different kind.

The free use of the terms "discrimination" and "reverse discrimination" are side effects of our use of "equality" to describe a broad range of situations, and of our preference for "equal rights" when arguing against injustice. When we want to call some practice unfair, we say it is discriminatory, just as when we want to call something fair we say it shows equality of treatment. What is needed is a clearer understanding of these terms and more care in their use; then it will be evident that there can be racial injustice without discrimination and racial justice without equality.

There has been enormous confusion about the two kinds of rights and their relation to equality. It would be nice to have one general principle, as Vlastos suggests, which both justifies some rights as equal rights and also justifies certain exceptions to them. The position I am developing is that there is no such general principle. We institute the rules and laws our conceptions of morality and justice demand, which is to say we develop them from within a moral context where issues arise. To claim that these have a deductive relationship with the principle of equality does not certify their justice; while showing a need that can easily be filled may be perfectly adequate justification.[15] Equality does not tell us what is just. But neither do we need a single principle to show us how to distinguish what is just from what is not. In contrast to Vlastos, I believe we have many "just making" reasons, and they can lead to a certain amount of moral uncertainty when we must choose among them. But the complexity is not optional. Neither a single principle nor a logical hierarchy of principles clearly exists.

If justice requires a mixture of special and equal rights, of course they cannot be just randomly related. We are constantly under the need to reconcile past rules with present ones and are trying to foresee future issues that may arise from our decisions.[16] Great effort is required to spell out the justifications and implications of social policies and the details of their application. But we need to see rights in their full and complicated nature, not to simplify them by means of a convenient concept like equality.

CHAPTER THREE Peers

The sense in which planks can be equal, and baskets of apples and pieces of cake, I call strict equality. It always involves a measure. But there is another kind of equality that pertains only to creatures in society, and this notion, though vague, is worth discussing. It is the sense in which people can be said to meet as equals and associate on equal terms. I will call this kind of equality the notion of "peers."

I

Although "peer" is often associated with membership in an aristocratic class, there is another side to its meaning. This has been emphasized in recent years by sociologists and psychologists, who use it to signify simply a relation between people. Such a relation is meant when Miss Moffatt, in the play *The Corn Is Green*, says to her former student as he is about to leave for Oxford: "For the first time we meet as equals"; they are no longer teacher and student, but peers.[1]

The roots of this idea are ancient. Aristotle, in his discussion of *philia* or friendship, links it with justice:

> For in every community there is thought to be some form of justice and friendship too; at least men address as friends their fellow-voyagers and fellow-soldiers, and so too those associated with them in any other kind of community. And the extent of their association is the extent of their friendship, as it is the extent to which justice exists between them.[2]

Philia covers a broad range of relationships, from casual acquaintances to lovers. Although we would not say that fellow travelers meet as friends, we understand that Aristotle is calling attention to a common feature of human relationships. People traveling together generally meet on equal terms: each is independent of the others but they share the common interest of reaching their destination. Similarly fellow soldiers, while they are not friends in our sense, meet as independent individuals who share a common interest. And like the fellow travelers, their relationship is a symmetrical one. They meet as peers.

According to Aristotle, friendship requires that the parties be similar in some important ways, and that they desire similar things from their relationship. "Bad men will be friends for the sake of pleasure or of utility, being in this respect like each other, but good men will be friends for their own sake."[3] So two thieves may be friends, but a thief and a virtuous man cannot: they are too dissimilar. Neither can a master, usually, be friends with his slave, nor can one in authority be friends with one under it. Not only dissimilarity is involved here; these relationships also prominently lack symmetry. Sometimes, Aristotle thinks, we can adjust for differences or asymmetries and compensate for them, and then friendship becomes possible. But they are none-theless obstacles.

The similarity necessary for peership changes from case to case and is difficult to specify. It can be grasped best, perhaps, by noticing some of the relationships where it is lacking. Many human relationships, as Aristotle recognized, are not those of equals, for example, the relations of parent and child, ruler and subject, master and servant. In these, the parties are dissimilar and stand asymmetrically to one another. In Aristotle's view the virtues of these relationships are different from those in the friendship of equals and not so valuable. Although one can say that parent and child have the "same interest," that is, the welfare and education of the child, this is very different from the similarity that characterizes two travelers, both wishing to get to their destination. The roles, if we want to use that term, are very different in one case, but alike in the other. The sense in which peers are similar is linked therefore to the condition of symmetry. Only in symmetrical relations will people meet as peers.

I use "peer" then to mean a relation between people with similar interests who associate and stand symmetrically to one another. As Aristotle says, comrades-at-arms are often related this way; so are children at play, especially when their ages and backgrounds are similar; while an elderly person and a youth cannot be peers, nor can a teacher and a student. It seems evident to Aristotle that neither can a husband and a wife.

Defined in this way, peership rests on the facts characterizing a relationship. A doctor and his sick patient are not related as peers, at least in the context of treatment. Neither, one would suppose, are a lawyer and his client; the latter depends on the former, and thus the relationship is asymmetrical. What if the doctor's patient is also his lawyer? It is reasonable to say that, since each kind of dependency prevents symmetry, the two together prevent peership twice over. But when the patient recovers and the physician no longer needs a laywer, it is then reasonable to suppose that they can meet as peers. This exercise shows that peership changes as the facts of a relationship change, that it is a kind of relationship holding between people only under certain sorts of conditions. A non-peer relation can in time turn into a peer one, and vice versa. Even Aristotle could allow that the freed slave might become the peer of his former master.

"Peer" is not a concept with sharp boundaries. People often meet as peers, as doctors do at a convention, only to arrive at a non-peer relationship on better acquaintance. This fits my characterization, for it shows that facts—and the knowledge of them—make a difference to such relationships. On the other hand it shows that peership may relate two people in one context but not in all the contexts where they meet.

It is very tempting to associate "peer" with social classes and social status, for this was part of its original meaning. Aristotle certainly thought that the best friendships typically concerned men who were both aristocrats, and that people of different classes would need some way of adjusting that difference if they were to be friends or peers. But in our society it is not clear what meaning should be given to social class or social status. A writer and an aviator may each command respect, but it is not respect due the members of a class. While both may have "status," that notion has a different meaning for each. A single hierarchy will not accommodate them. Nor does trying to associate peer with status clarify the term "peer."

The idea that a person should have a jury of one's peers, although it once meant a jury of persons of one's own class, found its justification in the fact that the outlook of someone in the aristocracy, his ethics and ideas of propriety, differed importantly from those of someone in the lower classes. It is therefore dissimilarity in outlook and standards, not simply the difference in class, that made "a jury of one's peers" important. And such dissimilarities as these are the ones I take to be relevant to my notion of peers. (It should be remarked that the Fourteenth Amendment does *not* guarantee that a person must be judged by a jury of peers in *any* sense. In Hoyt v. Florida [Sup. Ct. 368 U.S. 57, 82 S.Ct. 159, 7 (1961)], the Court said that the amendment "does not entitle one accused of crime to a jury tailored to the circumstances of the particular case." Otherwise a thief would have a right to be tried by thieves and a murderer by murderers. What it does guarantee is a jury randomly selected and thus representative of the whole society.)

My conception is therefore stronger than a notion of peer connected with class or status. If another concept were needed to explain it, the notion of "role" might serve, for it is being in the role of a teacher and in the role of a parent that prohibits our being the peers of our students and our children. But this idea is narrower than what I have in mind by "peer": the elderly do not have a particular role in virtue of their age, yet age does determine their non-peership with the young. Though the terms are vague and flexible, I shall retain the characterization of peer in terms of independence, similarity, and symmetry.

The relationship of parent and child is essentially asymmetrical. It will be a good relation when, as Aristotle said, "children render to parents what they ought to render to those who brought them into the world, and parents render what they should to their children."[4] Even as a child becomes adult, the relation connecting child and parent will usually contain asymmetries, some of them introduced as the parent declines. In contrast, a partnership of thieves may well be one of peers.

Standing in the peer relation with others is important and

valuable to us, and as Aristotle says, it introduces the notion of justice into social relations. Let us consider more closely how this relationship is connected with equality and the justification of rights.

II

An interesting problem arises here. As Aristotle valued the friendship of good and similar men as friendship of the best kind, we too tend to value peership as a model of good relations between members of society. Yet many of the most vital connections among people are not of this kind: children and parents, students and teachers, captains and crews, nurses and patients, legislators and citizens. If we value peer relations so highly, what follows for our attitude toward these non-peer ones? And if "peer" is taken to mean "equal," does it follow that these non-peer relations relate *unequals?*

First, remember that non-peer relations in my sense do not imply a difference in social status or class. Parents and their children are normally of the same class, and often so are doctor and patient, teacher and student, employer (in our society) and employee; though master and servant are commonly not. What determines peership is the way the parties stand, in their independence, similarities, and symmetry with respect to one another. For instance, two opera buffs or two scientists, two old people or two children, may relate to one another as peers regardless of their economic and social backgrounds.

In Aristotle's view, I remarked, a husband and wife could not possibly have the kind of friendship relating peers. The reason is that they are dissimilar in nature, and have different interests in their relationship. Since the relationship of husband and wife is, normally, asymmetrical, it will be usual in my sense too that husbands and wives are not peers. This description means no more than that the conditions of their relationship do not satisfy the conditions necessary for peership. And this fact derives both from the difference in conditions of life for the two sexes, and from the fact that sexual asymmetry or complementarity is an essential ingredient in the relationship. It is not just accidental or fortuitous that husbands and wives are usually of different sexes; that is part of the nature of the bond. Given this interpretation, I do not find anything pernicious in the conclusion that married people are often not united in a peer relation. After all, the sexes *are* different and those differences, some generated by roles in reproduction, have consequences for our perspectives. A union of individuals of opposite sexes which functions to raise children will necessarily contain asymmetries while childbearing concerns them. And this entails that the union is not, in that phase at least, one of peers.

Perhaps this needs further explaining. Given that a peer relation stems from independence, similarities, and symmetry, one can object that some couples *are* similar in just the kinds of features that would make us call them peers, were they of the same sex, both males or both females. Does sex alone prohibit their standing as peers? Peership works on different dimensions and admits of degrees. Such a relationship may share many characteristics with a peer relationship, and therefore might well be classed with them. A homosexual pair may be related as peers even though some dependency and subdued asymmetries characterize their relationship. As dependency, differences, and assymmetries become more pronounced, however, the peer relation turns into a non-peer one. To say that marriages with a function of childbearing involve non-peer relations is only to say that ordinarily the conditions for peership can't exist here.

It is not to say that the relation may not ever *become* one of peers. As the children of a marriage grow up and depart, and the attitudes and interests of a couple grow more similar—as they often do—something approaching peership often develops. There is no conceptual difficulty in this, just as there is none in the fact that elderly women in some tribes, well past childbearing and child-rearing, sometimes hold a position similar to the males and become, in that phase of life, their peers. As people's lives change, so do their relationships.

According to the idea of peership developed here, peer relations hold between individuals only where specific conditions are met. It is more common for relations to be non-peer or even ambiguous, neither clearly one nor the other, than to be peer. With relationships that are brief or tenuous it may be very difficult to say which kind they are; the relation of buyer and seller for instance is hardly a social relation at all, and not clearly identifiable either way. But it is clear that among non-peer relations will be some of the closest and most important ties that humans can have, with asymmetries that are marked, even dramatic. Compared to these, the relation of comrades-at-arms or that between two noblemen, however virtuous, will appear thin.

III

Distinguishing between peer and non-peer relations divides human relations into patterns. But does it help give us an interpretation of human equality? Since the dictionary tells us that "peer" *means* "equal," let us try substituting for "peer" the term "equal" and see what happens.

Difficulties arise at once. If peership is taken to be a relation of equals, it will follow that non-peers must be unequals. But how shall we understand this? Are a teacher and a student unequals—a lawyer and client, a doctor and patient? We want to ask: in what *sense* are they unequal? We can understand the notion of peer and non-peer relations without coming to any clear idea how equality is connected with it.

More curious still is the characterization of husbands and wives as unequals, though it is easy to see why they are generally not peers. How can inequality apply here? That parties are different and complementary, will justify saying a relationship is non-peer, but it is far from showing an inequality.

We are once more pushed around by the logic of our terms. If "peer" means "equal," then it seems that non-peers must be unequals. (Aristotle makes this inference, and backs it up with a metaphysics.)[5] But exactly what this *means* takes second place to its inevitability. As before, it seems harmless and even appropriate to say that two people are equals in some sense; but it is unclear what it means to say that two people are unequal, and, more than being unclear, it smacks of a dubious morality. We are faced again with the fact that no measure exists by which humans might be said to be either equal or unequal, and with our further reluctance to sanction any. Therefore, we should conclude, the terms "equal" and "unequal" do not belong here at all. Asymmetry is one thing, inequality is another, and while the former characterizes non-peers, it is difficult to see how the latter can. The consequence must be drawn that "peer" in the sense I have described cannot be translated as "equal." Nor is it any clearer than before what "human equality" can mean.

IV

The source of the idea of human equality, the philosopher David Ritchie says, lies in membership in a noble class:

[Our modern] ideal of equality is an inheritance from the inequalities of ancient societies; it is the idea of a peerage—an order or caste of nobles who recognize each other as in some respects and for some purposes equals, while asserting their superiority to the rest of the human race.

The idea that some men are equals has as its background the assumption that men are often unequal. But the "equality of men" was in time extended, and as it was, the background shifted.

The ideas of liberty and equality, once started, go farther. Even in the modern democratic ideal, there is no doubt that the equality of mankind is connected with the superiority of man as such to all the lower animals. . . . [This] alone justifies one in speaking of the equality of men as men.[6]

We could not speak of the equality of all humans unless we had in mind an inequality between them and something else. Human equality, therefore, has as its natural background other and inferior species.

That equality and inequality are synergistic, cooperating, terms is not surprising. But if Ritchie is right, the assertion of human equality provides no justification for rights. Asserting the superiority of men to animals does not indicate what rights men ought to have, or whether they should be the same for everyone. To say humans are equal in this sense is only to say that they are human.

Moreover, if we introduce my sense of peer into the proposition that men are equal, we get a result that is patently false. All humans *cannot* be peers. There could not be a society with only peer relations and without non-peer ones. Even the simplest society must have a variety of asymmetrical relations, husbands and wives, parents and children, a chief and a citizenry, and so on. A society of peers would not be a whole human society. It might be a band of hunters, or a group of women, or children of the same age at play, or a council of elders. A weird effect in William Golding's *Lord of the Flies* is that the entire community is of males who are roughly peers.[7] But a real society cannot be made up of individuals having only peer relations. To be composed of peers, it would have to be more than androgynous—it would have to be perfectly homogenized.

The character of non-peer relations is often unclear to us. A child may complain to its parents that it is not being treated as an equal, meaning that they are not treating it as a peer. That's right, and the reason is that parents and children *aren't* peers. Nor has a parent a choice about the relation; the fact of parenthood generates asymmetry. Again, students sometimes protest that they are not treated as equals, meaning that they are not treated as peers. Why shouldn't they be? Are they inferior? Their logic is moving, but the fact is they are not treated as peers because they are not peers. Put differently, for them to be treated as peers would vitiate the teacher-student relation; one cannot have both things together.

Often what is wanted when these protests are made is an appropriate form of respect. When that is the case, why not ask for respect in its own name?

Sometimes when women demand equality with their husbands, what seems to be wanted is peership with them. But this demand is difficult to interpret. If peership is to be possible, the conditions for it must be present: independence, similarity, and symmetry. If they are absent, the demand for peership is an impossible one.

Yet it may be objected that what is needed in the way of feminine equality is just those conditions that would make peership possible, conditions making peership between men and women a more general and common relationship. This means that women should be independent, have the same interests as men, and stand symmetrically in relation to them, for these are the relevant conditions. To the degree that these conditions are fulfilled, there *can* be something resembling a peer relation. For instance, there is something close to peership in childless marriages where both parties are engrossed in careers, and also in some marriages after children are grown. These are not conditions to be demanded, nor does a *right* to them make sense. But where asymmetries enter, reproduction being the most prominent, peership departs. Therefore in those phases of marriage where reproduction and the rearing of children are principal functions, there will be asymmetries preventing husbands and wives from being peers.

Rather than understand a demand for equality as one for peership, we may often better understand it as a demand for respect. It does not help to say "equal respect," notice, unless equality is definable. And where the parties are importantly different, equality of respect may be indefinable, like the equality of oranges and corn and that of dogs and cats.

To be treated as incompetent or irresponsible or has having only a childlike character is humiliating. No man would treat his peer that way. So it seems plausible that a wife needs just that role from which respect and dignity will follow, which is to say, she seems to need to be his peer. But that role may not fit her. Nor is it necessary for respect. Respect may rather need to be demanded in appropriate forms and in its own name.

v

Like Aristotle, we often view peer relations as models for good relations in a just community. These relations are ones we take as a standard, preferable to those involving dependency for instance. But since many valuable and necessary relationships are non-peer, is it perverse to value peership so highly?

Why do we identify peership with civilized human relations? The philosophers Rousseau and Hobbes recommended a social existence for human beings, pointing to the unbridled and ruthless competition which would exist in a "state of nature." There individuals would dominate and subdue and enslave one another to the limits of their strength and ability to prevail. The competition for dominance would be endless. Not only is this an unpleasant kind of life but it is morally offensive. Why should the strong profit inordinately from their strength? Surely human nature can aspire to something better.

When men come into society, having given their agreement, the society makes them equals, Rousseau wrote:

> Instead of destroying the natural equality of mankind, the
> fundamental [social] compact substitutes, on the contrary, a
> moral and legal equality for that physical inequality which
> nature placed among men, and that, let men be ever so
> unequal in strength or in genius, they are all equalized by
> convention and legal right.[8]

Society makes men equal, equalizes them. It may seem that society thus establishes men as peers, substituting this relation for those that are created in a competition for dominance.

Dominance competition and dominance relations are often used to characterize animal communities and sometimes, by extension, human communities as well. A "dominance system" is defined by the sociobiologist Edward Wilson as "in sociobiology, a set of relationships within a group of animals or men, often established and maintained by some form of aggression or coercion, in which one individual has precedence over all others in eating, mating, etc., a second individual has precedence over the remaining members of the group [etc.]. Dominance orders are simple and strict in chickens but complex and subtle in human beings."[9] In animal groups the dominant male usually has distinctive characteristics, by way of size or strength, personality or cleverness, and holds a position of some privilege, accepting tokens of deference from all other males and usually from females and young as well.

It is tempting to suppose that this kind of competition reveals inequalities among the troop members. Only the "superior" individual can rise to the top, and his superiority is guaranteed by the free competition that exists among males for such a spot. Robert Ardrey makes this inference. He believes that the suppression of competition for dominance among humans, fostered by egalitarianism, works against the advance of the society, for it restrains the power of superior individuals instead of giving their power full rein. "Inequality" is part of Ardrey's basic vocabulary; thus he defines a society as "a group of unequal beings organized to meet common needs."[10] The "alpha fish" or dominant member of such a community is superior and so *ought to* dominate, he argues.

There are plenty of difficulties with this inference from dominance to superiority, however. It is not even clear what "dominance" in such contexts signifies. Jane Goodall, for instance, wonders why the dominant position should be so desirable; the advantages it carries are often mostly formal.[11] Then there is the further problem why the male who achieves this position should be considered superior. Goodall relates the story of the rise of one chimp from near the bottom of the hierarchy to the top, not by virtue of strength or size or wit, but because he learned to make a ferocious din with empty kerosene cans as a technique of charging and challenging the others.[12] His "superiority" might be compared with that of Chico Marx. And Ardrey himself tells the story of a young female Japanese monkey that made a number of important innovations in her group's ways, yet whose status remained as low as ever. The story leaves one wondering whether dominance ordering has anything to do with intelligence or creativity or the progress they are associated with.

Another problem with dominance ordering is that in most species females do not even engage in a quest for a place on the same ladder as males. They will normally defer to the dominant male, whoever he is, and avoid the behaviors that characterize dominance competition in the male half of the community; at the same time they may have their own dominance ladder. What does this signify? Does it mean, as Ardrey supposes, that females are in general inferior—for otherwise they would rise to the top? Again we wonder if dominance can be taken seriously as a measure of superiority. How can one infer that females fail in a competition with males when they don't take part in it? It is interesting to speculate on why they don't. Midgley suggests that females do not need this kind of status as much as males because they don't get quarreled with so much.[13] But Ardrey might respond that this puts things backwards: they don't get quarreled with by males because they don't compete with males. For us the principal fact is that they don't compete with the males, and since they don't, the whole group cannot be ordered by linear dominance relations. That dominance ordering concerns only males is implied even in Wilson's characterization: for he says that the dominant individual has precedence over all others in regard to *mating*, which implies its application to only one sex group. The subjection of females is thus built into the definition.

It is unclear that dominance ordering gives us a measure of anything except the ability to become dominant, either in the male or female sphere. But while dominance ordering does not signify inequalities among individuals, not important ones, it does signify non-peer relations. Where individuals are related to one another by a dominance relation, it follows that they do not stand as peers.

It is very tempting therefore to argue that non-peer relations are essentially forms of dominance relations. The teacher has dominance over the student, it might be said, the doctor has dominance over the patient, the parent over the child. By analogy, the relation of husband and wife can be thought of as one where the stronger is dominant over the weaker.

To say this, however, is to read dominance into relations where that makes no sense. From the fact that a relation is non-peer, it does not follow that dominance is involved. Examples show that dominance often isn't. The relation of a teacher and student is not founded on a competition for dominance which, fortuitously, the teacher always wins. Neither is a doctor's position dependent on the ability to dominate. Indeed, that is incongruous: why would one expect *care* from someone in that position? And if parental authority signified only dominance, we would have to suppose that only quite aggressive individuals could satisfy the parental role. Finally, it is absurd to suppose that a female usually accepts a long-term bond with a male because he has literally conquered her (although this "cave-man" myth is sometimes taken seriously). Why would she accept such terms? Males of many species on the contrary work hard at winning the female of their choice, striving to impress and attract her, using all their skills and masculine assets. Among some primates, where there is no bonding to speak of, this characteristic is naturally less prominent. Courting and bonding go together. That males may become overbearing and autocratic is undeniable. That their success in dominating a would-be mate forms the basis of a long-term bond is ludicrous.

I construe "dominance relations," following Wilson, in a way that connects with human struggles for ascendancy, and so with the notion of status that grows out of them. If one were to construe dominance differently, so that the dominant male is primarily a protective and nurturing figure, then there would be greater similarity between dominance relations and non-peer relations in my sense. Furthermore the notion of "status" associated with dominance would be different. It is not quite so obvious under such a characterization where such alpha males are found in modern human communities.

Peership and dominance, although they are not linked as simple alternatives, are importantly related. And our preference for peer relations as the model for just relations in society has this connection at its root. It can be explained in this way: Although the non-peer relations of teaching and parenting and doctoring are important for a good society, they contain built-in hazards. Each of them is highly susceptible of abuse. Moreover, these abuses—parental abuse of a child, a doctor's abuse of a patient, a husband's abuse of his wife—are morally terribly offensive. Why is this? It is not, as it first might seem, that the offense is connected with dominance by one over the other. For if dominance were integral to the relations, they would not have the character they have: we would never let a doctor anaesthetize us, or take our lawyer's advice, or assume that our parent had our welfare at heart. No: what characterizes these relations is the trust that one party places in another. And it is this trust which makes the opportunity for abuse. The doctor, for instance, has charge of the medicine given a patient; how easy to do harm from this position! And parents receive great trust from their children; how easy that makes it for them to do harm! And it is likewise easy for a trusted husband to harm his wife; simple too for her to harm him. Trust makes these harms possible.

To identify these harms with abuses of power would be wrong. We do not feel the same kind of revulsion for one man beating another where both are competing for ascendancy. That is quite different from a husband's beating his wife, or a parent's beating a child; our revulsion at these springs from the trust which forms their background. The roles of doctor, parent, teacher, husband, wife involve trust so essentially that abuse of that trust is offensive in a way that no mere exertion of power can be. A parent who violates the trust entailed by having young children, we sometimes say, is no parent; the doctor who mistreats a patient is no doctor. Abuses of trust vitiate the very roles. And the harm that may be done here is deeper and more painful than any harm one peer can do another.

Peer relations are free of these hazards. While a slaveowner is responsible for his slaves, and a lord may be responsible for his vassals, freemen are not responsible for one another. The hazards of trust are absent, and it is perhaps for this reason that we prefer peership relations among people in a community. Why introduce the potential for abuse of trust where it is unnecessary?

I think *this* point is sometimes meant by the claim that men are equal and should be treated that way. It means they should not stand in relations of trust and responsibility where those relations can be avoided. Aristotle said that it is in relations between equals that we find justice among men. While the meaning of this remark was not clear at first, it can now be given an explanation; Justice can characterize peer relations as it cannot characterize most important non-peer ones. The mistreatment of a child by its parent is not simply unjust: it is morally reprehensible. To speak of justice and injustice in this context is inadequate. The issue is too deep for that. Aristotle said that justice does not apply within a family except by analogy with relations between equals, nor does it apply strictly to a man's relations with his slaves. He can be understood to mean that in those contexts the terms of paternal responsibility, affection, and care are more appropriate. Exactly this, it might be said, shows the chief wrong of slavery: it denies relations of justice between adults, creating great dependency where there need be none, and thus undermines the dignity of the slave's position.

Relations of justice are on a different level from relations of trust. To the latter, moral language is appropriate, and claims to rights have a curious ring—a child's "rights" vis-à-vis its parents, for instance, or a wife's vis-à-vis her husband. While with regard to justice, rights and contracts and predictable rules are not only appropriate but central. In dealing with one's peers, one should be able to anticipate, by means of laws and institutions, what will count as respectful and fair behavior.

In considering the rights women aspire to, this distinction is useful. For while rights are important in regard to the work place and dealings with institutions and laws, they can only indirectly affect the non-peer relations in which women stand, the most important being their relations with their husbands on the one hand and their children on the other. Wrongs that are present in these relations are more intractable than the others and harder to redress. They cannot be reached by an appeal to equality or equal rights, but need a searching understanding of the relationships themselves, our expectations of them and the roles that custom connects with them. Such relations need to be acknowledged as special ones, essential to and characteristic of a society, embodying its morality in ways that relations of justice cannot. They are deeper than peer relations, more perilous, and have a claim to moral priority.

VI

In setting forth the concept of "peer," I have tried to capture a sense of "equals" which enters our thinking about social justice, a sense in which individuals meet on equal footing. The term is admittedly vague in its common use, and often is taken simply to mean the troublesome equality we are trying to understand. By making it more specific I have tried to cast light on different patterns of human relations and the problems associated with them. And so I hope to shed light on our attachment to the idea of equality.

Peership failed to satisfy our need for a relation which might relate all members of a society and give us a sense of human equality. Peers must be independent and similar and their relations symmetrical, and many human relations lack these features. They are non-peer relations. Nor are they rightly viewed as inferior to peer relations and less desirable; on the contrary they include the closest and most essential of all human bonds. Moreover, there could hardly be a society made up entirely of peers unless it excluded different generations and all relations built upon trust. Trust is an essential feature of the most important non-peer relations, carrying with it the potential for abuse, for betrayal of that essential trust. In the face of this danger we generally prefer to meet others on equal terms, as peers. But such a choice is often not open to us. We can create democratic institutions, structured so that individuals meet as peers within them, but we cannot create a democratic family whose members are peers.

The notion of "peer" is associated in our minds too with the absence of dominance by one party in a relation. But although dominance relations are non-peer, non-peer relations often do not involve dominance. It is absurd to characterize parent-child relations, teacher-student relations, and husband-wife relations as essentially involving dominance.

With this exploration we put aside the search for a meaning of equality that satisfies the equalitarian principles, and turn to consider how rights are in fact supported, how in law equality enters their justifications.

CHAPTER FOUR

Gender and the Law

Among rights, some are equal and some are not. The question how to justify the one kind without jeopardizing the other has no general answer. But if we look at some Supreme Court decisions regarding women's rights, we begin to see how the two kinds of rights and their justifications can be fitted together.

I

On the one hand, not all rights should be equal; in some areas and for some purposes justice requires that rights be different. On the other hand, Aristotle's claim that likes should be treated alike and unlikes treated differently provides no guide either. People are different in their racial characteristics, among others; does this justify treating them differently? While Aristotle would say that some social differences reflect differences in people's souls, we are not prepared to go so far. We may need to be content with saying that some differences among people justify some differences in treatment, while for some rights nearly all differences are irrelevant.

The problem of women's rights has this two-sided form. In regard to some rights we want to say that sex is an important difference and ought to have a bearing on rights. With respect to others we want to say that it is unimportant and, like race, ought to be entirely ignored. Is there a single principle by which the two kinds of rights can be sorted out? We should be prepared to accept that there may not be one.

Some rights obviously should be equal. In a case that came before the Supreme Court in 1971, an Idaho law was challenged because it provided that when two persons of different sexes had comparable claims to be appointed administrator of an estate, the male candidate should be chosen over the female.[1] The appelant sought appointment as administrator of her son's estate in preference to the child's father, from whom she was separated. She argued that her rights under the Equal Protection Clause of the Fourteenth Amendment were violated by the Idaho law, since that clause guarantees equal protection of citizens under the law regardless of race and sex. She argued that she was entitled here to the same treatment as a man, and that her qualifications as administrator should not include her sex.

The Supreme Court agreed with her, judging that "by providing dissimilar treatment for men and women who are thus similarly situated, the challenged [law] violates the Equal Protection Clause."[2] But the key words here, as in Aristotle, are "similar" and "dissimilar." The Court had previously and consistently recognized the power of the States to treat different classes of people in different ways. What the Equal Protection Clause denies to States, it had held, is

the power to legislate that different treatment be accorded to persons placed by a statute into different classes on the basis of criteria wholly unrelated to the objective of that statute. A classification "must be reasonable, not arbitrary, and must rest upon some ground of difference having a fair and substantial relation to the object of the legislation, so that all persons similarly circumstanced shall be treated alike." [Royster Guano Co. v. Virginia, 253 U.S. 412 (1920)][3]

With respect to administering the estate of their son, two parents might be similarly placed and qualified, or one might be better qualified than the other: these are the relevant considerations in designating an administrator.

The Idaho law suggests that women are generally less qualified than men to administer an estate. But no evidence was given to support this. And nothing intrinsic to being a woman suggests females *must* be unqualified. Therefore it seems obvious that the right should be an equal one. The Court added that classification by sex here makes "the very kind of arbitrary legislative choice forbidden by [equal protection]; and whatever may be said as to the positive values of avoiding intrafamily controversy, the choice in this contest may not lawfully be mandated solely on the basis of sex."[4] Arbitrary classification by sex might make administration easier for the courts, but this is not adequate justification for the differential treatment.

This is an exceedingly clear case in which women should have the same rights as men. Some other cases with a similar outcome involve laws that are outdated, that may have once been appropriate but now put an unfair burden on women in the name of "protecting" them. Examples are laws that prohibited women from working overtime, and laws restricting the weights women can lift: these often work simply to exclude women from well-paying jobs they are quite capable of doing. At the Senate Hearings on the Equal Rights Amendment to the Constitution in 1970, Myra Harmon (then president of the National Federation of Business and Professional Women's Clubs) testified:

We believe that the term "protective" no longer applies to this kind of legislation. Certainly at one time special labor

regulations for women were protective because these were
the only labor laws on the books.... Today the sweatshop
conditions, the dawn to dusk hours, the subsistence level
pay are to a large degree sins of the past.... Thus, women
do not need protection against oppressive conditions which
have ceased to exist. They need the same things men workers need.

Once such "protective" laws may have been reasonable,
Harmon argued, in part because laws protecting men did
not exist. Times have changed; men are now protected and
women stand to suffer from the extra restrictions.

Special labor legislation for women restricts as fully as it was
originally intended to protect. These laws prevent women
from competing on equal terms with men.

If the working rights of men are extended to women by
removing from the books laws pertaining only to women,
women stand to gain. They will have a better chance at
well-paying jobs. Harmon continued:

We submit that such legislation creates distinctions between
men and women, which in light of prevailing industrial conditions and the contemporary state of medical knowledge,
are arbitrary, anachronistic and unreasonable.[5]

Harmon's view is interesting, partly in acknowledging
that our perception of what is fair may depend on an understanding of the laws and institutions and how they work.
With different social conditions, differences in law are justified, and the existing laws and practices form part of her
argument. An abstract question of equal rights is not involved here. Therefore the equal rights she argues for differs from the right to vote and serve on juries, for the latter
are *not* grounded in facts, nor are they susceptible to change

with changing social conditions. *They* might plausibly be seen as deriving from a general principle of equality; the right to work without differential treatment cannot be. Nor does Harmon appeal to the intrinsic justice of equal treatment for men and women:

> What must be demonstrated is that a particular weakness in women requires the particular kind of restraint which is being imposed. With labor laws for women it should be asked whether the restriction is reasonable, given first, the physical capacity of women, and second, the industrial conditions which prevail in the particular industry to which the law is being applied.[6]

An argument for restricting women's rights needs to turn on facts relating to women and work conditions, not on an abstract principle. To "protect" women by excluding them from well-paying jobs is, by common perception, high irony.

A curious example of a "protective" law was a Michigan statute that allowed a woman to obtain a bartender's license only if her husband or father were owner of the bar. The law was challenged by a female bar-owner who claimed that it violated her rights.[7] The Supreme Court disagreed with her claim to equal protection, saying:

> Michigan evidently believes that the oversight assured through ownership of a bar by a barmaid's husband or father minimizes hazards that may confront a barmaid without such protecting oversight. This Court is certainly not in a position to gainsay such belief by the Michigan legislature.[8]

The Court held that a state has a right to make laws protecting its citizens and a legitimate concern with the "moral and social problems" that bartending by women give rise to. A woman's right to equal protection does not override this.

The appellant viewed the doctrine of equal protection as an abstract guarantee that she would have the same rights as men. The Court disagreed. But equal protection (like human equality) cannot be supposed to entail that all rights are equal. By contrast, Harmon, in attacking protective laws, might have argued that the courts should consider the circumstances under which a law operates and the fairness of the consequences it gives rise to, and that courts and legislators should use these to determine what rights are needed. Arguing in that manner might, indeed, have been more persuasive. While granting the right of a state to protect its citizens, it could emphasize that the law which was intended to protect women, actually adds to their burdens. In restricting them economically it fosters their dependence on men and therefore their vulnerability. Whatever real protection it might purport to give is more than offset by these negative consequences. In sum, then, the law is not protective. For this argument, no principle of equality or equal protection is needed; moreover the main issue—the harmful consequences of the law—is rightly identified.

Consider another appeal to equal protection. Sharon Frontiero, a lieutenant in the Air Force, sought housing and medical benefits for her husband as a dependent. She found that, unlike a man seeking the same benefits for his wife, she had to prove her husband's financial dependence for more than half of his support. Her husband took the case to court arguing that he was unfairly discriminated against. He also argued that classification by gender, like classification by race, is inherently suspect and, if used, needs some powerful form of justification. The Air Force's defense was that the policy was instituted for reasons of "administrative efficiency," on the assumption that by and large wives are dependent on their husbands and not vice versa.

The Supreme Court had little patience with this defense and quoted the Reed opinion that "the Constitution recognizes higher values than speed and efficiency."

Any statutory scheme which draws a sharp line between the sexes *solely* for the purpose of achieving administrative convenience, necessarily commands "dissimilar treatment for men and women who are . . . similarly situated," and therefore involves the "very kind of arbitrary legislative choice forbidden by the [Constitution].[9]

However, the Court did not declare sex an "inherently suspect" classification, as it had with race. (Three concurring judges explained that this was not done because, first, it was not necessary, and, second, the Equal Rights Amendment, if passed, would make sex classifications suspect without the court having to pass judgment on it.)[10] The determination whether legislation that distinguishes treatment of the sexes involves "arbitrary" distinctions was therefore left to be considered case by case.

The issue of "administrative efficiency" in the Frontiero case is connected with stereotypes or standard ways of thinking about the husband-wife relationship. It reminds us of John Stuart Mill's picture of "coequality," an idealized version of human relationships by reference to which laws and principles could be shaped. But not only are stereotypes transient and inclined to be dated; they are also inherently treacherous. Even supposing that 99 percent of the wives of Air Force personnel are economically dependent on their husbands, does this justify placing an additional burden on a couple who depart from the pattern? The use of stereotype generalizations in law can be disturbing, as the following cases bear witness.

Martin Marietta Corporation had a practice of screening women with preschool children from certain of their application lists, but they did not screen men in this way.[11] The appellant Phillips argued before the Supreme Court that the policy therefore violated her right to equal treatment, showing a bias against women. The company said it had no bias against women; the preponderance of women in the category at issue showed as much. Although the Civil Rights Act prohibits discrimination in employment on the basis of race, sex, color, religion, and national origin, it adds that sex, religion, and national origin may be used as criteria where there is a "bona fide occupational qualification reasonably necessary" to the business or enterprise.[12] So the Supreme Court argued, the "existence of such conflicting family obligations, if demonstrably more relevant to job performance for a woman than for a man, could arguably be a basis for distinction."[13] But was there such a basis? The Court said the evidence wasn't clear either way and refused to grant Phillips her claim.

But what evidence would have satisfied the Court? The Court said that it would have been moved if there were proof that "some women, even the vast majority, with preschool-age children have family responsibilities that interfere with job performance and that men do not usually have such responsibilities".[14] The criteria, the Court added, must be neutral as to the sex of the applicant, apparently meaning that they must be expressible in sex-neutral terms. Even so, this stipulation is hardly reassuring. As Justice Marshall observed, this opinion allowed the Supreme Court to be influenced by stereotypes regarding women's proper role and qualified the intent of the law, which meant that exceptions should be made only in special forms of employment, as, for example, actors, actresses, and fashion models. His dissent observed that two kinds of issues needed resolution: the relation of stereotypes to ostensible job qualifications, and the relation of facts about a group to the treatment of an individual in it. Both issues were to arise in other cases.

For instance, the issue of sex stereotypes and job qualifications came into focus in a suit by male applicants for jobs as airline attendants, who claimed they were discriminated against on the basis of sex.[15] Pan Am did restrict hiring to females; the question was whether being female was a bona fide occupational qualification. A lower court found Pan Am's policy to be justifiable on grounds of women's superior performance in "providing reassurance to anxious passengers, giving courteous personalized service and, in general, making flights as pleasurable as possible within the limitations imposed by aircraft operations."[16] Part of the evidence consisted of passenger preference and the superior ability of females to take care of the "psychological needs" of passengers. The trial court allowed that some men could no doubt perform as well, but that "admission of men to the hiring process, in the present state of the art of employment selection, would have increased the number of unsatisfactory employees hired, and reduced the average levels of performance of Pan Am's complement of flight attendants."[17] The lower court supported the airline, therefore, arguing that "to eliminate the female sex qualification would simply eliminate the best available tool for screening out applicants likely to be unsatisfactory and thus reduce the average level of performance."[18] But the Supreme Court supported the appellant, saying that Pan Am could not "exclude all males simply because most males may not perform adequately."[19] And even though the public preferred female attendants, the Court found that this preference was based on stereotype thinking rather than actual performance differences; and in any case, it said, customer preference could not be used to justify sex discrimination.

Here the issues of stereotypes and average performances are connected, particularly in the attitudes of passengers. But if we separate them, it seems much clearer that stereotypes are a poor indication of job abilities than that group characteristics are. If there is incontrovertible proof of sex differences, can one nevertheless argue that they should be disregarded?

One interesting case involved the argument that women

should have equal rights with men, not because they are alike, but *because they are different*. It concerned a Louisiana law providing that women should not be selected for jury duty unless they filed written declarations that they wished to be. As a result, many women were not on the jury lists and juries were overwhelmingly male. Suit was brought by a woman on trial for killing her husband; she claimed that the composition of the jury and the law that led to it, created conditions for sex bias and an unfair judgment against her.[20] The Court said that her claim was right:

> The selection of a petit jury from a representative cross section of the community is an essential component of the Sixth Amendment right to a jury trial.[21]

But if there is no difference of any importance between the sexes, and if Justice ought to be blind when it comes to sex, how is it important whether women sit on juries? Justice White, who wrote the majority opinion, faced the issue squarely. He argued that "women are sufficiently numerous and distinct from men that if they are systematically eliminated from jury panels, the Sixth Amendment's fair cross-section requirement cannot be satisfied."[22] But isn't this to say that the sexes are importantly different and may differ in judgments about what is just? Precisely. White wrote:

> The truth is that the two sexes are not fungible; a community made up exclusively of one is different from a community composed of both; the subtle interplay of influence one on the other is among the imponderables. . . . The exclusion of one may indeed make the jury less representative of the community than would be true if an economic or racial group were excluded.[23]

The sexes are not fungible—that is, they cannot take each other's places. They are too different. But then, what is being argued for is not so much an equal right as fair jury composition. Women are needed on juries *because they are women*, and because they are different, their representation is a necessary condition for the jury system to be fair. It is implied that in this capacity men cannot represent women, nor women men. Both perspectives need to be represented, and this means, represented by members of each sex.

The justifications for equal rights in the cases above range widely: one uses a premise that women are no different from men (e.g., in the ability to administer an estate); one concedes that women and men *may* be different, but argue that equal rights should be granted anyway (as in the Pan Am case); and the last case *emphasizes* the difference between men and women as an argument for representing both points of view. If men were substitutable for women on juries, as they are in the administration of an estate, there would be no argument for their "equal" right to serve. But they are not substitutable, according to White, and their interplay is an important "imponderable" of society. We need the balance of these two viewpoints. And in the need to be distinctively represented, the court found sex groups to be *unlike* economic classes and racial groups. The differences of sex, it implies, go deeper. Their assimilation to one position is not thinkable.

Equal rights, then, are argued for in a variety of ways. Sometimes they rest on provable similarities, sometimes they are justified in the face of differences, sometimes they even depend upon differences. Would it help if there were a principle of equality from which all are derivable? The answer must be no. For the justifications of equal rights are not all the same, and no principle comprehends them all.

II

Where the differences of sex is relevant to a right, say, in the case of a right to maternity leave or medical coverage for pregnancy, claims to equal rights can interfere with rational ways of arguing. This happens in Geduldig v. Aiello, where the appellant demanded that the disability insurance of the State of California ought to be made to cover maternity expenses, because in not doing so it discriminated against women.[24] The Court disagreed and declared with sly logic that there is "no risk from which men are protected and women are not. Likewise there is no risk from which women are protected and men are not."[25] The protection being the same, it is naturally equal. The Court elaborated:

> The program divides potential recipients into two groups— pregnant women and nonpregnant persons. While the first group is exclusively female, the second includes members of both sexes.[26]

Since nonpregnant persons include women as well as men, the policy could not be called *sex*-discriminatory nor said to violate the Equal Protection Clause.

This reasoning is both amusing and rather grotesque. A medical insurance program needs to cover some disabilities which pertain to both sexes and some which pertain to only one sex. For example, the California program covers prostatectomies and other difficulties pertaining only to men. To say as the Court did that women have the same right to this benefit as men puts "equal rights" in a useless role. How does a woman have this right? Is it potentially hers in the event she should become a man? The attempt to speak of special rights as if they were equal leads, as we saw earlier, to very odd ways of talking about rights. Better to say that men have some rights not applicable to women. This lays the ground for arguing that women should have some rights not applicable to men.

The specific claim needed is that maternity coverage should be included in the insurance program, not because it is something everyone needs but because it is needed by some women. How can such an argument be made? That is the question.

In fact the crux of the Court's decision in Geduldig was not equality of rights or the question of sex discrimination. Rather it was the cost of including maternity coverage in the health benefits program, which would lead to a large increase in the cost of insurance to each worker. The court said:

> It is evident that a totally comprehensive program would be substantially more costly than the present program and would inevitably require state subsidy, a higher rate of employee contribution, a lower scale of benefits for those suffering insured disabilities, or some combination of these measures.[27]

But if this is the real issue, one wonders that the Court should undertake to decide it. Might it not be better decided by the employees themselves? The costs and the benefits could then have been balanced by those who would pay for and benefit from them. In any case, the idea that "equality of rights" can settle an issue like this is an illusion.

As I have argued, arguments for rights often cannot be made to depend on an abstract or general principle. If, for example, there is a need for education for the retarded, should we appeal to a *principle* to say what kind it should be, how much there should be, and how much money can be spent on it? There are fiscal issues to be balanced against others: for instance, how much money is needed and available for educating normal children, how much for care of the elderly, how much to support fatherless families, and so on. Recognizing a need and setting about to address it does not determine how much help should be given. We would probably agree that educating retarded children should not detract substantially from the education of normal children; nor should medical help for the terminally ill place undue burdens on those who are healthy. The cost of rights is relevant to their institution. But how are the lines regarding expense to be drawn? Would it be of any help to try to formulate general lines without regard for funds or circumstances? It seems unlikely.

Apart from raising the question of cost, the Geduldig case shows the limitations of egalitarian arguments. To say men and women have the same rights to something that only one group can possibly use is specious. Just as a woman cannot have a right to a prostatectomy neither can a man have a right to maternity care. If there are rights to these things they are, by their nature, special rights.

Gender differences and special rights were also the issue in the case of Kahn v. Shevin.[28] There, a widower sued the State of Florida because gave a tax exemption to widows which it denied to widowers. This, Kahn argued, was sex discrimination and unconstitutional. But the Supreme Court disagreed:

> There can be no dispute that the financial difficulties confronting the lone woman in Florida or in any other State exceed those facing the man. Whether from overt discrimination or from the socialization process of a male-dominated culture, the job market is inhospitable to the woman seeking any but the lowest paid jobs. . . . The disparity is likely to be exacerbated for the widow.[29]

Acknowledging differences in the situations of widows and widowers, the Court said that the law was "reasonably designed to further the state policy of cushioning the financial impact of spousal loss upon the sex for which that loss imposes a disproportionately heavy burden."[30]

Are classifications by gender "suspect"? In the Kahn case, the Court thought they could be "benign." But how do we decide whether they are benign or not? Justice Douglas, who in Frontiero argued in favor of labeling sex classifications suspect, here went with the majority. He proposed to reconcile the disparity of his two opinions as follows:

> Gender had never been rejected as an impermissible classification in all instances. Congress has not so far drafted women into the Armed Services. [Moreover the Court relied on a brief emphasizing that] the physical structure of women has a bearing on the conditions under which she should be permitted to toil.[31]

That two reasonable opinions by a thoughtful and sensitive justice stand in logical conflict shows how inadequate equality is to deal with the issues raised by sex differences. If gender classification is not always suspect, what point is there in calling it suspect at all? What Douglas is saying is that some rights *should* relate to gender and some should not. But he does not explain how his commitment to equal rights can be reconciled with this position.

Interestingly, the widower in Kahn was supported by women's rights organizations, which apparently perceived less threat from the insensitivities of equal rights and equal protection than from the differential rights which so long worked to women's disadvantage. One can understand this concern. Nevertheless it is a fact that widows in general do have a much more difficult time than widowers, and that the severity of their needs justifies attention by the state just as the needs of others do. A woman who has for years attended to a home and family often finds herself in later years in an uncompetitive employment position. Can it be denied that this inability to compete for the necessities of life is a legitimate concern of society?

In the E.R.A. hearings, Senator Bayh repeatedly asked

witnesses whether they perceived a possible conflict between equal rights and rights which pertain to women distinctively. He asked Harmon, for example:

> Are you concerned at all about those laws whose thrust, it
> seems to me, could not be changed inasmuch as some laws
> are aimed directly at the attributes of women as distinct
> from males, such as laws providing maternity benefits or
> those relating to criminal assault against women? Do you
> foresee such an impact [by E.R.A.] on this type of law?[32]

To which Harmon answered:

> It seems to me these are special aspects of our life and would
> require special laws. For instance the maternity laws are
> provided to help the extension of the human race and not
> [just women]. . . . If a man could bear children he would be
> under the same law as a woman is.[33]

These are "special aspects of our life," she says, but not
special aspects of women's lives. To bring them into the
form of equal rights she makes them applicable to pregnant
men as well. It is comical reasoning. Aileen Hernandez,
president of the National Organization for Women, answered a similar question from Bayh in stronger, but not
clearer, terms:

> Maternity benefits are not a sex benefit. They are medical
> benefits for some women who are about to become mothers,
> and motherhood, it seems to me, is a different kind of con-
> cept and a legitimate benefit.[34]

Motherhood is "a different kind of concept," she says. Different from what? Is motherhood some kind of anomaly?
Not only maternity leaves and maternity costs are associated with motherhood, as Hernandez appears to

suggest. For many women there is a substantial part of their adult lives devoted one way or another to caring for families. Can no rights relate to this? Is this whole form of life anomalous? These are the kinds of questions raised by Kahn. If in this case "equal rights" makes sense, then a great deal in our everyday lives fails to.

There is a persistent inclination shown in the testimony of women's rights representatives to say that things are best made and kept equal. One witness declared:

> After the Constitution is amended the presumption will be that every difference in treatment between man and women [*sic*] [is] prima facie discrimination, rebuttable only by a showing that such treatment is functionally necessary. Men alone may be considered for jobs as attendants in the men's rooms of the Capitol, but not for positions of President of the United States, Secretary of Defense or Justice of the Supreme Court.[35]

The matter of eligibility for political office is easy to grant. But the statement quoted also seems to imply that preferential treatment for widows, in lacking a justification on "functional" grounds, would therefore be unjustified. Harmon too, when Bayh asked about a divorced husband's responsibility for child support, replied:

> The husband and wife should be equally responsible for the education and upbringing of a child... the woman ... just as responsible in this area as a man, both in the mental and psychological upbringing of the child as well as the earning power and support of that child monetarily.[36]

If mother and father had the same share of each kind of responsibility and similar roles, she seems to say, then justice would be tantamount to equality. Hernandez too sees the "right" solution as one defined in terms of equality:

In my opinion all alimony laws, to the extent that they talk about "wife" and "husband" as opposed to "spouse," and therefore differentiate between the two, solely because of sex, should be changed to read "spouse" everywhere. I think that it is obvious that women who are capable of working, who are divorced, should not be getting alimony payments from their husbands, but should be supporting themselves.[37]

Both these remarks ignore the issue raised by Kahn that women who rear children are at a disadvantage when, in later years, they seek work in competition with both men and younger women. It does not serve their interest to change "wife" to "spouse"; on the contrary, that change would put aside recognition of whatever social contribution they have made outside the work place. The chief advantage of Hernandez' proposal to speak neutrally of "spouses" is that it holds us to a simple guide for constructing arguments about women's rights, and that guide is the familiar principle of equality.

When Bayh asked Hernandez specifically about women who have spent much of their adult life at home caring for a family and who are then divorced, she observed:

There are, of course, some problems when you get into marriages which have been going on for years and years and years, where one of the spouses has been depending on the other to support him or her. I think that in those cases there would probably have to be provisions made for the spouse who is incapable of earning a living because of total lack of experience and preparation to be provided for by the other spouse who has been supporting him or her.[38]

The phrase "him or her" does not disguise the fact that Hernandez is speaking of the needs of older divorcees. By conceding that there "would probably have to be provisions," she admits, albeit reluctantly, that there will need to be special rights to support, not only equal ones. And thus the potentiality of conflict between the justifications and scope of both kinds of rights is implicitly acknowledged by her statement.

Of course the reasoning for women's rights would be made clearer and simpler if there *were* greater overall similarities in the situations of men and women vis-à-vis remunerative employment. And many feminists advocate making the roles as similar as possible, even to advocating that women with young children *should* also be pursuing careers in roughly the same way men do, so as to enhance the similarities of the roles of the sexes. But this plainly puts such women in a double bind: they have the responsibilities of women at home *and* the roles of working men. Is this not a reductio ad absurdam of equality? Then too, marriages that go on "for years and years and years," while they may work against making the sexes similar, need not otherwise be such a bad thing.

Speaking of "him or her" as if the sexes are the same will not convince us that they are. And if institutions and laws are made for a sexless species, they will obviously not fit the two-sexed one we belong to. Can we then insist that people accommodate their lives so that the difference of sex *will become* negligible? But that certainly is a Procrustean bed. To some the price required by this "equality" will seem absurdly high.

III

Sometimes it is clear that sex should make no difference to rights while sometimes it clearly should. And in still other cases it is not easy to say what to make of it, to say which kind of consideration should guide us. Of the last type is the case of L. A. Water and Power v. Manhart.[39]

Mary Manhart worked for the Los Angeles utility, which required women employees to make larger contributions to the pension fund than males on the ground that women on the average live longer than men. Manhart protested that this is a form of discrimination against women; for the same coverage, the same amount per month on retirement, women must pay more than men. There was no dispute about the facts. As the Court explained, the case

> involves a generalization that the parties accept as unquestionably true: women, as a class, do live longer than men. The Department treated its women employees differently from its men employees because the two classes are in fact different.[40]

The question was not whether the actuarial tables were accurate but whether they should be used in this way. How was the Court to decide? On the one hand "equality" could be used to justify equal payments into the fund for equal sums payed out of it; on the other hand "equality" of benefits received—over the individual's lifetime—could justify *un*equal amounts paid in. It is a difficult problem *how* to express it in terms of measures, for they can cut both ways.

The Court argued that classification by sex in regard to pension payments does not adequately respect individuals.

> All individuals in the respective classes do not share the characteristic which differentiates the average class representatives. Many women do not live as long as the average man and many men outlive the average woman. The question, therefore, is whether the existence or nonexistence of "discrimination" is to be determined by comparison of class characteristics or individual characteristics.[41]

The Civil Rights Act of 1964, the Court argued, made it "unlawful to discriminate against any *individual* with respect to his compensation, terms, conditions, or privileges of employment, because of the *individual's* race, color, religion, sex or national origin. " The statute therefore "requires that we focus on fairness to individuals rather than fairness to classes."[42]

But any characteristic can be used to define a class. What the Court seems to say then is that *no* classes can be drawn in this regard. Its idea of respect for the individual really amounts to ignoring all individual characteristics and treating everyone alike. The pension plan should therefore be blind as regards individual characteristics. To call this "focusing on fairness to individuals" is of course curious.

The issue as the Court viewed it was whether the insured group should be broken into risk-classes at all.

> Healthy persons subsidize medical benefits for the less healthy; unmarried workers subsidize the pensions of the married workers; persons who eat, drink, or smoke to excess may subsidize pension benefits for persons whose habits are more temperate. Treating different classes of risks as though they were the same for purposes of group insurance is a common practice which has never been considered inherently unfair.[43]

Would it be fair for smokers to pay higher medical insurance rates than nonsmokers, and lower pension rates? It is currently common to make high-risk drivers pay more for automobile insurance than others, and in a number of areas, people deemed to be low-risk are given preferred rates. Is it clear that these classifications are unfair?

Suppose we admit that they are fair. There remains another argument against using sex classifications in the same way. For the distinctions above concern behavior that a person chooses to continue or not, while sex, like race and place of birth and nationality, are matters we have no choice about. To classify people on these lines would seem to us unfair simply because they are fated.

Yet one can imagine that insurance rates might take such characteristics into account, showing that descendants of the Scottish live longer on the average than descendants of Swedes, and people born in Cleveland live longer than those born in Los Angeles, and that rates are determined accordingly. In that case, having one's rates determined by being a female of Swedish descent born in Los Angeles, would not be in principle more unfair than having rates determined by the last two factors alone. The fact that other categories of fated characteristics are *not* used now is one of the reasons for saying that classification by sex also should not be. The reasoning here is therefore relative. (My views here follow roughly the lines set out by D. Z. Phillips and H. O. Mounce, who argue that a moral judgment has force only within a system of practices, a form of life. Change that background and the force of a judgment or the rightness of it may change too. Moral judgments on this view cannot rightly be taken in the abstract and they are not deduced from general principles.)[44]

Pension payments that go up for a group when women are added to it constitute a problem against a prior background of rates set for males alone.[45] If the pension costs to both workers and employers increases as more women are hired, isn't this a good argument—to both—for not hiring women. And then, to other grounds for bias against women, there would be added their longevity! That this consequence is pernicious is a good argument, it seems to me, against insurers breaking down the insured population by sex classes. But it is such an argument because present institutions and practices and business economics do give rise to unfair treatment of women in a variety of ways, and the pension-payment differential adds to them. It is not intrinsic to classification by sex that it is unjust.

IV

Some of the rights needed by women, especially some connected with jobs and promotions, are equal rights. Some of the rights needed, especially those relating to women who care for a home and family, are special ones. There is no one rationale for them all. The justifications have to be worked out case by case. For some issues the biological and reproductive differences of the sexes play a crucial part, but in others these differences need to be carefully ignored. Because the sexes are not, for some important purposes, interchangeable, sex bias is of a different order from racial bias. There is no general argument in favor of assimilating the sexes as there is for assimilating the races. And some of the appropriate arguments for representing women acknowledge the importance of their distinctive needs and points of view, which is not the case with race.

Ronald Dworkin observes of affirmative action programs:

> Affirmative action programs seem to encourage . . . a popular misunderstanding, which is that they assume that racial or ethnic groups are entitled to proportionate shares of opportunities, so that Italian or Polish ethnic minorities are, in theory, as entitled to their proportionate shares as blacks or Chicanos or American Indians. . . . That is a plain mistake: the programs are not based on the idea that those who are aided are entitled to aid, but only on the strategic hypothesis that helping them is now an effective way of attacking a national problem.[46]

His view is that affirmative action programs are instruments for achieving a better society, which will thereafter not need them. As in the good society that Wasserstrom describes, the just state will ignore differences of race and national origins. But while this instrumental concept of affirmative action works for race, it does not work for sex.

Even in the good society there will not be eventual assimilation or the ignoring of sex differences. Therefore, if there is an argument for representing women because they are women, for example on juries, then that argument will not become useless in a better society. On the contrary, a really good society may be expected to encourage representation of women in a variety of areas, with the idea that their viewpoints *should be* influential.

Because the rights wanted and needed by women are diverse and have various justifications, it is extremely hard to give a summary set of programs for a "women's movement." On the other hand, general terms are too thin. In the Senate hearings on E.R.A., Congresswoman Florence Dwyer said:

> Women want only what is their due. They want to be treated as whole citizens. They want to be recognized as having a full stake in the life of our nation. Consequently they also want the means necessary to fulfill this role: the right to earn a living and obtain an education, to make a contribution equal to their talent, to receive the job and promotional opportunities commensurate with their talent, to provide an equal measure of security for themselves and their families... [and] participate fully and equitably in the public and political life of their community and country.[47]

If this statement concerned racial groups it would be understood that what is wanted is the roles and rewards possessed by others. Inasmuch as it concerns women, the phrases are ambiguous: "to provide an equal measure of security for themselves and their families"—does this mean equal to what men have? And then does it imply that men provide it for themselves *and their families?* But as some women are counted in these, *their* interest is joined here with that of men. The problem is one of translation: Are women asking for the same opportunities and rewards as men, or for some that are different? Are their circumstances assumed to be the same as those of men or not?

Ambiguity about the nature of the goals is evident again in this remark by Congresswoman Margaret Heckler:

> Women are not requesting special privilege—but rather a full measure of responsibility, a fair share of the load in the effort to improve life in America.[48]

Does this mean: Women do not want special privileges but they may want special rights? Do they want a full measure of responsibility but not necessarily the same responsibilities as those of men? The answer might be: They want appropriate rights and respect, which may or may not be similar. Heckler also observed:

> The average woman in America has no seething desire to smoke cigars or burn the bra—but she does seek equal recognition of her status as a citizen before the courts of law, and she does seek fair and just recognition of her qualifications in the employment market.[49]

Although Heckler acknowledges that women do not on the average want to mimic men, she leaves unclear what "equal recognition" means. What form should it take? Must it have the same form as for men? If not, then the word "equal" is hardly apt. Women want recognition and respect and some forms of protection. For working women, this may mean equal treatment, but for nonworking women, another understanding of these terms is necessary.

Gender *does* make a difference in law, and, in making a difference, makes for confusion in the law, confusion that turns largely on the weight given the concept of equality.

How can we have equal rights which are also differential? How can there be equal recognition if it is not the same in form? The old questions about similarity now arise in regard to rights. The way out of the confusion, I suggest, is to distinguish some rights as differential, not equal, and to allow that these as well as equal rights can be justified.

CHAPTER FIVE

A Two-sexed Species

The idea that sex differences are or should be negligible is curious. Nor can it be explained just by looking to arguments about rights; its roots are deeper and more various. What makes us suppose that sex differences can be ignored?

I

At the other extreme from supposing that sex differences don't matter is the belief that gender is closely associated with a host of tastes, skills, manners, qualities of temperament, and habits of mind, as if sex determined a wide variety of unrelated characteristics. Such a vision of sex differences is suggested in Hawthorne's *The Marble Faun:*

There is something extremely pleasant, and even touching—at least, of very sweet, soft, and winning effect—in this peculiarity of needlework, distinguishing women from men. Our own sex is incapable of any such byplay aside from the main business of life; but women—be they of what earthly rank they may, however gifted with intellect or genius, or endowed with awful beauty—have always some little handiwork ready to fill the tiny gap of every vacant moment. A needle is familiar to the fingers of them all. A queen, no doubt, plies it on occasion; the woman poet can use it as adroitly as her pen; the woman's eye that has discovered a new star turns from its glory to send the polished little instrument gleaming along the hem of her kerchief. . . . The slender thread of silk or cotton keeps them united with the small, familiar, gentle interests of life, the continually operating influences of which do so much for the health of the character, and carry off what would otherwise be a dangerous accumulation of morbid sensibility. A vast deal of human sympathy runs along this electric line, stretching from the throne to the wicker chair of the humblest seamstress, and keeping high and low in a species of communion with their kindred beings.[1]

Girls are taught to sew and mend and embroider; at least they were in the times represented, while boys are not. But Hawthorne thinks that teaching is connected with deeper differences that would reveal themselves in any case. Female nature and this distinctive interest in needlework are intimately bound together, never mind how. Of course the writer who finds women thus sweet, soft, and winning is an appreciative male; a woman author would hardly write in the same way. Such sex stereotyping in literature is hazardous, however beautiful the prose. To women who don't sew, the vision may be anomalous.

The polarization of the sexes need not be romantic. Otto Weininger gave to the complimentarity of male and female natures the form of a strange psychological theory. He writes:

The real female element has neither the desire nor the capacity for emancipation in [the sense of moral freedom]. All those who are striving for this real emancipation, all women

who are truly famous and are of conspicuous mental ability,
to the first glance of an expert reveal some of the anatomical
characters of the male. . . . [They] have almost invariably
been what I have described as sexually intermediate forms.[2]

Women's fundamental concern is with sex, Weininger
theorizes, while men's natural province is the world of intellect and morals. He quotes approvingly the saying, "the
longer the hair, the smaller the brain,"[3] and he says this of
equality:

> It is most important to have done with the senseless cry for
> "full equality," for even the malest woman is scarcely more
> than 50 per cent. male, and it is only to that male part of her
> that she owes her special capacity or whatever importance
> she may eventually gain.[4]

The sexes are too different, the female too inferior in, and
unconcerned with, intellect for sexual equality to have any
meaning. And exactly the sensitivity and feeling that
Hawthorne extolls, Weininger deprecates.

> [The] want of definiteness in the ideas of women is the source
> of that "sensitiveness" which gives the widest scope to vague
> associations and allows the most radically different things to
> be grouped together. And even women with the best and
> least limited memories never free themselves from this kind
> of association by feelings.[5]

As women are inferior to men, so are feelings inferior to
intellect.

Women's identification with sexuality is derivative from
the sexual character of both men and women, Weininger
acknowledges. It is men's sexuality that makes women into
sexual objects, and gives rise to women's identification with

what is sensual. Therefore if women are to be treated as full human beings—as equals—men too must be free of sexual interest. But this will lead to the extinction of the race— well, then it will.

That the human race should persist is of no interest what- ever to reason; he who would perpetuate humanity would perpetuate the problem and the guilt, the only problem and the only guilt.[6]

Weininger believes that sexual desire leads men to treat women as objects, which conflicts with both our reason and morality. For women to be emancipated and become edu- cated to something better than they are now, it is necessary that sex cease to relate the sexes. But with this change there will also be a transformation in women's nature: "A woman who had really given up her sexual self, who wished to be at peace, would be no longer 'woman.'"[7] The final moral resolution involves banishing sexual relations between the sexes and the consequent loss of women's original nature. This is another argument for androgyny.

The difference of sex, as Weininger sees it, gives rise to a moral problem concerning sexuality and the use of women as objects, and from this, guilt arises. The guilt has no resolution within a sexual framework; hence sexuality itself needs to be banished. In various forms this theme haunts Western culture. Moral innocence and sexual awareness are incompatible. Weininger's view adds to this theme ambiva- lence about female nature and whether it is really alterable without becoming the same as the male. In such ways as this, moral theory and psychology become entwined. (That a moral concept like guilt naturally enters psychological theory is also plainly evident in Freud.)

A question Hawthorne and Weininger both leave us to puzzle out is the extent to which sex differences and sexual nature are independent of culture. We can change our culture; and supposing we do, to what degree would our natures remain intractable? Margaret Mead demonstrates the wide variability of forms that relations of men and women can take. From the gentle, unassertive, child-nurturing Arapesh, to the noisy and assertive Iatmul, to the artistic Tchambuli—the contrasts between male and female virtues, roles, and personalities change radically.[8] Among the Tchambuli, for instance, where sons were especially treasured and men freed from many practical concerns, "the minds of small males, teased, pampered, neglected and isolated, had a fitful fleeting quality, an inability to come to grips with anything." The small girls, on the other hand, were more alertly intelligent and enterprising. By contrast, the Mundugumor tribe, which is more egalitarian, raises children to be "independent, hostile, vigorous," producing boys and girls with similar personalities.[9] Ah-ha, notes the egalitarian, sexual equality is possible after all! Not so clear:

> In such a society, women are handicapped by their womanly qualities. Pregnancy and nursing are hated and avoided if possible, and men detest their wives for being pregnant.... Women are masculinized to a point where every feminine feature is a drawback except their highly specific genital sexuality, ... [even] to a point where any aspect of their personalities that might hold an echo of the feminine or maternal is a vulnerability and a liability.[10]

Precisely what one would expect. Sex egalitarianism leads to sexual uniformity and this means the suppression of whatever does not conform to some neutral or masculine norm. In a professedly egalitarian society like ours, one where pregnancy is also increasingly optional, a woman might conclude that it is best avoided. Yet this general form of sexual arrangement is clearly not viable.

With her observation that sexual roles are almost incredibly malleable Mead might be expected to support the assimilationist ideal and that of a more or less androgynous society. But she does not.

A one-sex world would be an imperfect world, for it would be a world without a future. Only a denial of life itself makes it possible to deny the interdependence of the sexes.... We must think instead of how to live in a two-sex world so that each sex will benefit at every point from each expression of the presence of two sexes.[11]

The moral problems sex gives rise to need to be dealt with, she implies, but not as Weininger would—by abolishing sexuality and sexual distinctness. They need addressing within a two-sex framework.

Sex roles are malleable: that is not in dispute. The question is how to make decisions about altering them. What kinds of considerations should guide us? If we are committed to an egalitarian form of society, then our decisions will be guided by a vision where the roles of men and women will be indistinguishable. But such an arrangement may not find answering resonance in our nature—on the contrary, our nature may constitute an obstacle and something this vision has to strive against. If, on the other hand, we start with the assumption that some differences in roles will exist, and then ask how to balance them justly—what latitude is possible within them and where the community should provide support—then our options are wide and interesting. Such a starting point seems intuitively reasonable. As Midgley wrote, "we can vary enormously the forms [the roles of the sexes] take and our own individual part in them. We can no more get rid of them than we can grow wings and tusks."[12]

II

We like to think of our species as lacking an important division of the sexes. Why is this? Weininger gives part of the answer: We think of humans as a species of a very well-endowed kind, essentially governed by reason. Animals operate from instinct and drives, but humans think and evaluate and are self-conscious, and so are morally responsible for what they do.[13] This nonanimal, reasoning part of us is distinctive of the species. In the language of theology this higher part is a soul, or sometimes a rational soul. In either conception, secular or religious, that part of human nature stands in contrast to the physical or animal nature. Over that nature it is expected to be the passionless governor, holding sway, though often tenuously. Plato observes that such an uneasy bonding creates a continual struggle which ceases only with death. The most powerful image of this concept is contained in the *Phaedrus*, where Plato describes the condition of the individual in terms of a charioteer struggling to control his two horses, of which one is black and unruly, the other white and reasonable. In the *Republic*, however, he views reason as the governing part of every human soul, so giving to *it* the role of the charioteer.

The rational self, this higher passionless part of us, is of course sexless. Sexuality along with appetites and the physical necessities of life belongs to the lower, animal part. But it follows directly from this that sexuality is not an important part of our nature, nor is sexual identity an important aspect of identity, nor is even reproduction an important feature of human existence. All that sexuality entails is rather to be conceived as a distraction from our proper human concerns; and those are spiritual, rational—and so, androgynous.

The Christian view of humans is egalitarian. According

to it men and women are intrinsically human souls, intrinsically alike. Which is to say they are sexless.

This is a very deep-rooted view of ourselves. What would happen if instead we considered ourselves as *essentially* sexed, not just in body and superficially, but deeply? Suppose we imagined that differences of sex affect our attitudes and perspectives. In that case the entire distinction between mind and body would start to fray, yield, and dissipate. What would a female as contrasted to a male soul be? The question might make sense in other cultures and religions, but it does not in ours.

III

Let us try to view human beings without a mind-body prejudice and count our species as one among others, allowing for the possibility that its sexual character may be interesting and important for understanding it *as* a species, with the manifold relations that exist among its members. This view means that, when we come to deal with sex roles and their justice, we should try to understand the respect we owe our nature.

In describing a species of creature, one begins with the most outward features: its habitat is such a place, its food is this and this, its life-span so long. For the purpose of these general descriptions, sex differences can mostly be ignored. Next there are such features as migrations, traditional places for breeding, spawning, and rearing young: for some of these too sex may be irrelevant. Next we need to describe the changes characterizing the species with respect to its transition from childhood to adulthood, from the transient immature forms to the stable adult one. For *this* description, distinctions of sex will generally be crucial. The young male develops in such and such way, the female in another. The male grows larger horns or brighter feathers, grows bold at danger; his calls are louder, he competes with others males. The female develops mousier colors and quieter ways, and her cycles proceed with such-and-such timing. Without mentioning differences of sex, the description of development would be impossible, because maturity comes to the sexes in different ways. Next we come to the areas where sex enters most dramatically and essentially, the areas of courting and mating, gestation and bearing (or hatching), and the rearing of young. Here we obviously need to speak not only of sex differences but of sex roles. How does the female, heavy in pregnancy or tied down to her nest, manage to sustain herself and protect herself from enemies? If food is plentiful and in easy reach, and if enemies are rare—as with the Gombe chimpanzees—she may survive without help. If conditions are less comfortable or enemies abound, she will need help from a mate. *Which* mate? The one that wooed and joined with her earlier, helping to build a nest or find a cave in some apparently instinctive pattern of cooperation.

It is hard for us to describe humans in an analogous way, in part because we do not think of reproduction as so important in our lives. We are not in such a degree controlled by it; on the contrary we have control over both our social institutions and our reproduction in a degree unknown to any other species. We are deliberate and foresighted (and rational) and not the passively helpless victims of either biological or environmental forces. Does this mean that there is no answer to the question, how does *our* species manage its mating, reproduction, and child-rearing? If there *were* an answer, would that be a sign of our irrationality?

Consider some of the patterns of sex roles in other social and intelligent species. The langurs of India, for example, form themselves into two kinds of groups, one containing all females plus a single dominant male, the other containing less dominant males. The band containing all the females also contains young, most of whom are fathered by the leader male. To copulate with a female an outsider must invade the leader's group, risking discovery and challenge. But such males are free to rove and wait their chance, while the leader of the female band must be watchful, protecting his troop both from enemies and from threats to his leadership. His protective and fatherly role has one particularly interesting qualification. When he takes over a troop, the dominant male will kill any unweaned infant. At this the bereaved mothers go into estrus and the male fathers a new generation of his own line. Apparently his father protection is connected with offspring of his own blood line.[14]

Chimpanzees by contrast are more loosely structured. While males often travel in bands, roving into neighboring territories, the females stay with the slower-moving young through a long childhood, and the young get only occasional help from an adult male. Males are free to copulate with any female in estrus that accepts them, though dominance order is observed. Understandably there is not much meaning to the role of father. Instead, close connections are generally formed among siblings, and between mothers and children. Even grown males may return to the maternal nest when their lives become difficult.[15]

Gibbons, in contrast to both of these two species, form themselves into monogamous families which often endure many years.[16] There may be "affairs" between one member and an outsider, as there are among geese, who are also monogamous. (Konrad Lorenz describes how a gander may have "affairs" of long duration with a female and yet never treat her with the respect he accords his mate, or guard her nest or acknowledge her offspring).[17] But families tend to be stable, and both parents care for the young. Neither has a very keen or active interest in sex.

Wolves are more family-minded even than these. A

father wolf is especially protective of his young and solicitous of his mate, feeding them both at the expense of his own appetite.[18] Even supposing that in the rigors of its environment the wolf has an instinctive drive to help his mate and young survive, the tenderness of the father wolf is still unaccountably warm.

This is only a small sample of the various ways the sexes relate in species of social animals. But it sets the stage for the question how *our* species compares with others in its sex roles—what is our pattern?

There is little agreement among scientists about the answer. Margaret Mead observes that we are unique among primates in having an important paternal figure. In the case of most primates "the male does not feed the female. Heavy with young [the female] fends for herself. He may fight to possess or protect her, but he does not nurture her." In contrast to these, human males are distinctively nurturing:

> In every known human society, everywhere in the world, the young male learns that when he grows up, one of the things which he must do in order to be a full member of society is to provide food for some female and her young.[19]

Although this father role is a distinguishing mark of humans among primates, it is a learned rather than an instinctive response. Society teaches boys in this way of life, Mead says. And so the characteristic is fragile. Although it is "a primary condition of [our] humanity," it can be lost. "We hold our present form of humanity on trust," Mead infers.[20] Her view is particularly interesting for the light it casts on the egalitarian's disparagement of sex roles, and makes us ask: Would relations between the sexes be really more just without this important and distinctive role of father?

In contrast to Mead, the animal ethologist Irenäus Eibl-Eibesfeldt argues for a causal connection between the nurturing human father and our sexuality. Sexual arrangements serve the need human children have for long years of protection and education, he proposes:

> Nature has apparently used up all the possible means of forming and maintaining a bond [between human mates]. Apart from the group-uniting mechanisms... nature has made considerable use of sexual behavior for the purpose of maintaining heterosexual partnerships. The need to make use of this possibility probably arose because of the length of the period of... development in man.... [For many years, the mother] needs the division of labor in which the man gives her help in the procuring of food and, in particular, protection. For this reason she must tie him to her emotionally for a long time. The tie afforded by the sexual drive is therefore particularly suited to this because it is very strong. On the basis of the fulfillment of a sexual desire a bond can be easily cemented. This presupposes, however, that the woman can respond to the man's sexual desires most of the time, something that calls for new and special adaptations in the physiology of the woman.[21]

This account is curious. The author proposes that a male will stay with his family and protect it only if he is rewarded in terms of other satisfactions, namely sexual ones. He has no interest in his offspring as such, unlike the gibbon and the wolf, and needs to be bribed into responsible behavior by the rewards of sex. An unflattering view of human males. The human female, on the other hand, identifies her interests with those of her young, offering herself sexually to the male as the price of her and her young's security. It is not a pleasant representation of the "highest" species. Moreover, being thus related to desire, the arrangement is fragile and will come apart if the female is not readily available to her mate. Compared to this, the sex lives of other animals appear as models of temperance.

If the relation between sexuality and sex roles is difficult to explain in animals, much more is it in humans. Consider the biological innovation of our species, the lack of estrus cycles as a determinant for female receptivity. Eibl-Eibesfeldt sees this adaptation as one needed by the long term of child-nurture, but this does not tell us what happens to the role of the female who is thus "adapted." A female of any other species can refuse the advances of a male without hesitation—she is not ready, she is not interested. But human females commonly find this difficult, as if they needed a very good excuse. They are *supposed* to be ready and interested. Why? Is this a mark of a higher species? Is it supposed to follow from their lack of estrus that they are always ready? Obviously it doesn't.

The human sexual arrangement, instead of being simpler than that of other species as Eibl-Eibesfeldt suggests, is more complicated. According to Mead, while before marriage a female has the right to say yes or no to sex, "in marriage all this is changed.... It is his unperiodic, insistent desire that sets the stage, not her more fitful moods."[22] It is difficult to understand the female's role and status. They cannot be understood simply as the price women pay for long-term bonding and fatherly protection of children. That bonding is not guaranteed to be long-term in any case, and children need not be part of this picture. As Mead says, it is a confusing role. Also on the male's side, the bond must be seen as more than simply sexual. Mead characterizes its complicated nature:

> From the moment that actual long matings between human beings develop in which male and female live together, and her receptivity is such that she is accessible to his desire at any time, a host of new problems face human beings. The male's achievement as a lover becomes tangled with his need for a wife, with his tie to the children whom he has learned

to nurture, with his standing in the community. While the primate needs a female for immediate physical reasons and for no other, a human male... needs a wife.[23]

Mead implies that the mating bond is not formed simply for sex (as Eibl-Eibesfeldt says); rather sex makes difficult the bond which is formed for other reasons. Compared to those of animals sex roles of humans contain a variety of such difficulties and confusions and conflicts. That may be their most distinctive character.

Jane Goodall, unlike both Mead and Eibl-Eibesfeldt, emphasizes the similarities between humans and chimpanzees, saying that "sexual relationships between male and female chimpanzees are in large part similar to those that can be observed among many young people in England and America today."[24] Like Mead, she sees the nature of the long-term relationship of sexual mates as most distinctive of us:

> The obvious difference between [chimpanzees and men] lies in the fact that men and women are capable of establishing and maintaining monogamous relationships both physical and spiritual of long duration, and this sort of bond is not known in the chimpanzee.[25]

But this does not mean humans are all monogamous, or that most are always so. They have a tendency like chimps to promiscuity. And like chimps, fathers—even responsible ones—often spend much time away from their families in the company of other men. Also the mating picture has been affected by women's demand for equality in some countries, she says, where the result is "free love" and "large numbers of unmarried mothers."[26] Like Mead, she sees the monogamous and stable pairing of humans and the distinctive role of the father as changeable features of our species. We might as "naturally" gravitate toward the pattern of chimpanzees.

The picture we get from Mead and Goodall is that of a species whose character is rather unclear. It is characterized on the one hand by the fatherly role of the male parent, but not consistently; it is characterized on the other by a tendency to promiscuity, but most noticeably among the young and among single males. Therefore it seems difficult to say anything very general about our nature except that for humans sexuality is a mighty concern and that responsible fatherhood is a tendency stronger for us than for other primates but less strong than it is for wolves.

Perhaps then it is most characteristic of humans that they feel divided, ambivalent, pulled in conflicting ways. That is the conclusion Mary Midgley comes to, and not only with regard to sex roles.

> We are fairly aggressive, yet we want company and depend on long-term enterprises. We love those around us and need their love, yet we want independence and need to wander. We are restlessly curious and meddling, yet long for permanence. Unlike many primates, we do have a tendency to pair-formation, but it is an incomplete one, and gives us a lot of trouble.[27]

We are unsettled and creatures of conflict. We have deep motivations going in opposite directions. For such creatures a commitment may be difficult.

> No *long-term* commitment is ever always easy and unforced. And no commitment involving more than one person ever suits all parties equally. Yet human nature certainly demands long-term enterprises. We are therefore bound to be frustrated if we cannot finish them, so commitment is necessary.[28]

Among our long-term enterprises is the rearing of children. But more than this, we bind ourselves in marriage because we *want* long attachments. We don't just accept them as the price of something else, sex or children, she argues.

> We want deep and lasting relationships. And because these are often difficult, we "bind ourselves" in all sorts of ways to go through with whatever we have started, even when it proves annoying. Marriage is simply one of these arrangements.[29]

The answer to why we have such an institution is, then, that we want it—not just something else to which it is the means. The desire for pair-formation among humans is not derivative from the desire for children but is strong on its own. Midgley says, "Pair-formation could never have entered anybody's head as a device deliberately designed to promote utility.... Individuals want to live in pairs before they have any children, and continue to do so when their children are gone."[30]

Other forms of conflict also go deep, Midgley believes.

> Let us consider the predicament of primitive man. He is not without natural inhibitions, but his inhibitions are weak.... He does horrible things and is filled with remorse afterwards. These conflicts are prerational; they... [fall] between two groups of... primitive motives... They are not the result of thinking; more likely they are among the things that first made him think.[31]

Instead of one rudimentary conflict between reason and the animal self, a number of diverse conflicts pertain to human nature, and reason may be brought in to help deal with them. Even at best, this account suggests, resolutions will be temporary. The nature we live with is essentially divided.

Midgley's representation of human nature explains why psychology and morality should be intertwined. She writes: "Only a creature of this intermediate kind, with inhibitions that are weak *but genuine* would ever have been likely to develop a morality." We have inhibitions, but they are not as strong in motivating us as they are in other creatures; they need reinforcing. "Conceptual thought formalizes and extends what instinct started."[32] We reason because we need to, and we need to because we are ambivalent.

These four natural scientists hold different views about the character of the human species, and about its sexual and social character in particular. While Eibl-Eibesfeldt sees male humans as egoistic, needing special incentives to mate monogamously, the other three see humans as basically social, the need for pairing a deep one, however unreliable. But it is striking that all four agree in the perception that sex differences are important, not just in respect to the process of reproduction, but in a multitude of other ways. Nor does society play an incidental role in the development of sex differences. Rather it has a productive and essential part. From the mother chimpanzee, a young female learns how to care for her own young, and without that learning may not be an adequate mother. From other males, young males learn to copulate, something animals brought up in isolation may never learn to do.[33] With humans too there is learning connected with our adequacy as sexual beings. Mead goes further, claiming that society has credit for creating fathers of male humans, teaching them in this role which is then identified with our "higher" nature. Midgley sees culture as an essential part of our nature, needed to "complete" us, and not something that stands in contrast to what we are. Nor on her view can sex roles or sexual identity be separated from what we are. They are bound up with our motivation, our conflicts, and so our most fundamental character.

The roles of males and females in different species may

be very stylized, and often the *point* of the role contrasts is far from clear. Among birds, for instance, there will be one species in which only females build nests, and another in which only males do, and another in which both cooperate. Within a species there is great uniformity, but among species there is very great variation. This difference seems clearly to show that part of the roles identified with sex are arbitrary. In part they are roles that creatures of either sex could perform as as well as the other. Here is an argument for equality, for androgynous roles. One feminist writer, Jane English, characterizes sex roles:

> "Sex roles" and "gender traits" refer to the patterns of behavior which the two sexes are socialized, encouraged, or coerced into adopting, ranging from "sex-appropriate" personalities to interests and professions.[34]

Sex roles are imposed upon us by culture and education. Without them we would be more free and our lives richer in possibilities. Another feminist writer, Ann Ferguson, defends androgyny:

> I shall argue that male/female sex roles are neither inevitable results of "natural" biological differences between the sexes, nor socially desirable ways of socializing children in contemporary societies. In fact, the elimination of sex roles and the development of androgynous human beings is the most rational way to allow for the possibility of... love relations among equals, and... development of the widest possible range of intense and satisfying social relationships between men and women.[35]

Ferguson goes further, claiming that "human babies are bisexual and only *learn* a specific male or female identity by imitating and identifying with adult models."[36] Gender identity is entirely a creation of society, she seems to say; biological differences could be virtually dropped out.

Sex roles are not entirely the result of natural differences, and in many respects they are only indirectly related to reproduction. Furthermore, some of the characteristics of one sex role *could have* characterized the other. This is tantamount to saying that in some sense sex roles are largely arbitrary. But is this the same as saying they are largely indispensable? Does it mean that no reason exists against dispensing with them? That isn't obvious.

Consider that human infants need a great deal of care, and care of certain kinds. They also need education in a variety of things if they are to survive in this, or in any other, environment. Someone has to teach them, and it is reasonable to suppose that one parent or both should help to do it. Now, caring for and teaching children are roles, which is to say, these in turn need to be taught. To whom should they be taught? In view of the fact that mothers are the primary parents, bearing young with or without an acknowledged father, they surely need to learn something of child care, just as they should know something about pregnancy and childbirth. But then it does not follow that men should *not* also learn. If they did learn, moreover, their involvement would not exemplify an *absence* of roles. Parental roles *are needed*. Nor does it dispose of the underlying asymmetry of parenthood.

The attack against sex roles is commonly made in rather Rousseau-like terms—society corrupts and perverts man's nature, and would do better to leave us alone. But this objection to child-care roles is silly. A human who relied entirely on instinct in these matters would be taking grave risks and acting with unnecessary individual responsibility. Even young animals learn about the care of infants by observation; we can hardly do less. But this learning *is* the learning of a *role*. Such roles are beneficial and necessary.

The egalitarian protest is more plausibly made against the sex-differentiated aspect of parental roles. Why should *only* women learn child care, why not men too? One traditional answer is that, since women must learn it, men should be exempt. But of course this doesn't follow. If only women learn the role, their options to do other things will be severely limited, while if men learn it as well, their options will not be greatly impaired. A cooperative conjunction of child-caring roles may be an optimum solution for both men and women. While releasing women to pursue their careers, it may also improve men's lives in their roles as fathers, since in this way they become more familiar with the offspring they are formally encouraged to love and protect. All around, a sharing of child care may enrich the lives of both parents, and probably of children as well.[37]

To accept this solution is simply to accept that—since some sex roles can be changed—parenthood and its skills need not be left exclusively to women but should be taught to men as well. This shift, however, would not make the roles androgynous. Consider, if both men and women are taught about the delivery of a baby, and both are taught to "participate" in it, their roles will still be sex-differentiated. And similarly, there will be some sex-differentiation in parenthood. But there will be greater cooperation between parents on this score than is found in most Western societies, and that is an important improvement.

To train both men and women in parental roles is not to banish roles but to change and enrich them. Nor is it clear that we would be any happier with fewer and leaner roles. Midgley says that "social animals cannot live the life they are fitted for at all without their own form of society. The demand for it is as deeply inherent as the demand for one's own future safety."[38] She goes further:

Forms and ceremonies are not idle. "Stereotypes" ... are utterly necessary. And they are *not*, as people often unthinkingly suppose, merely means to an end, devices that any "intelligent" being would naturally hit on for reaching a few, simple, physical ends like food and shelter. In the first place, half of them are not means at all; they are ends in themselves. The joys of friendship and affection, and also of hatred and revenge, jokes, dancing, stories and the whole business of the arts, games and other play, disinterested curiousity, and the enjoyment of risk are natural *tastes*, things that make life worth living, not things that could possibly have been invented as a means to staying alive.[39]

She suggests that we *need* roles as we need a culture, though it is not a need connected with survival. We will not die without them. Nevertheless, games and dancing and story-telling and a great variety of things natural to all people involve roles. Why disparage them as a class?

Suppose the objection is narrowed so that it is directed simply against those social sex roles which are not connected with reproduction. These, it might be argued, are inherently pernicious for they serve to divide and separate the sexes, thus encouraging differences of status. If we cannot have a completely androgynous society (the argument would go), at least we could reduce the amount of difference between the sexes to its minimum. But it is not altogether clear that minimal sex roles would serve us well, and to Midgley's voice we can add Mead's:

If society defines each sex as having inalienable and valuable qualities of its own but does not relate those qualities to the reproductive differences between the sexes, then each sex may be proud and strong, but some of the values that come from sex contrast will be lacking. If women are defined without reference to their maternity, men may find that their own masculinity seems inadequate, because its continuance into paternity will also lose definition.[40]

As we are born with sexual identity, we need its definition in social terms, and particularly we need recognition of its connection to parenthood and reproduction. For these matters, she seems to say, constitute a fair part of what life is *about*. This recognition means, however, the introduction of precisely the kind of sex roles that feminists object to. The nonfunctional and functional aspects need to be tied together, Mead proposes.

Reproduction is left out of the recommendation for androgyny. That is logical because androgyny is primarily concerned with relations between adult males and females. It is for such adults that "love relations among equals" and "development of the widest possible range of intense and satisfying relationships" are advocated. "Mere reproduction," like "mere biology," is irrelevant to this image of the good society. But for some people, important "love relations" will include those between parent and child, to which, in turn, "the widest possible range of intense relationships" is meaningless. There is a difference in life view or perspective involved here.

The most powerful argument on the side of androgyny and against sex roles is the egalitarian one. If sex roles interfere with equality, as Ferguson and English and Wasserstrom believe, then, *if* equality is an important moral goal, this is good reason for saying that sex roles are bad, even though we like them and find them natural. If giving up games and story-telling and dancing were necessary in order to achieve a better society, we would at least have to give some thought to their eradication, and probably make a serious effort in that direction. Midgley writes: "We could, after all, quite plausibly say that friendship or sport or the arts threatened freedom;... [but] this would be a bad reason for abolishing them altogether."[41] One might answer that it depends on how serious the threat was. But we have seen that equality does not offer us a clear vision of society at all, much less of a good society. In the absence of a compelling reason against them, it seems reasonable to suppose that sex roles in some form or other are tolerable. What is needed is not their abolition or their amalgamation to a single androgynous role, but adjustments within them. In many respects adjustment is needed to make the roles more similar. For females to be stereotyped as unintelligent and illogical and unable to make serious commitments shows ignorance of the lives most women lead. It is literally false. To base role differences on these supposed differences is consequently unfair. But to say that grown women are generally somewhat easier with children than men, somewhat more expressive of feelings, more understanding of others' feelings, more demonstrative, and somewhat less competitive, is not clearly false. Nor are the consequences for sex roles clearly negligible. Some differences between the sexes, their nature, temperament, and roles, may actually be a nice thing.

IV

The thesis that androgyny is a good model for human society depends on the assumption that males and females are, for all reasonable intents and purposes, alike. Differences between them, it is maintained, are chiefly due to culture and conditioning. If sex roles were abolished we would see the similarities stand sharp and clear, where now they are muddied by roles and stereotypes. Thus Jane English argues:

> Of course it may be true that there are some personality differences between the sexes in any case, regardless of social pressures ... to conform. With the present evidence, however, since there is no stereotype-free society available to observe, we cannot establish scientifically whether such biological or innate differences exist.[42]

But there *are* studies establishing sex differences between infants that may account for some personality differences.

For example, there is evidence that girl infants are more sensitive to touch at birth. From this difference it has been inferred that females "also have a greater reactivity to physical stimuli," and that this greater tactile sensitivity is "a necessary precondition for empathy and imagination."[43] The inferences seem exaggerated even if some difference is granted. Yet there are other differences less disputable, for instance, the greater maturity of females at birth and their earlier arrival at puberty. Then there is firm evidence that girls excel at verbal tasks at school, and evidence that their brain development is somewhat different from that of males.[44] Are these differences interrelated?[45] The subject is fascinating to physiologists and psychologists. What is sure is that sex differences exist from infancy which are not the result of conditioning.

Evaluating a vast array of studies, two psychologists, Eleanor E. Maccoby and C. N. Jacklin, disclaim the judgments that girls are more social than boys, more suggestible than boys, better at rote-learning and simple repetitive tasks; and that boys are more analytic, more affected by environment, and more motivated than girls. Among differences they find "well established," however, are: girls have greater verbal ability than boys; boys better visual-spatial ability and, as they mature, better mathematical ability than girls; and boys are more aggressive. Maccoby and Jacklin specifically disclaim the inference that socialization may be responsible for differences in intellectual abilities and in aggressiveness. The latter, "cross-culturally universal" and susceptible to change by sex hormone treatment, they argue, is clearly related to sex.[46]

There is evidence that concrete differences exist between the sexes besides the reproductive ones. What does this show? It shows first of all that society does not create all those differences that are not directly connected with reproduction. On the contrary; it suggests that we should allow for various differences between the sexes and not adopt single linear scales for distinguishing all individuals regardless of sex. It suggests that men and women of talent, for example, will not generally match on the same set of parameters, and therefore, if a single standard is assumed and if that should be drawn from a sample of males, the comparison with a sample of women may be invidious. It will produce a bias against women while it is defended as an "objective measure" of ability. One often hears that women candidates for important offices do not "measure up" to the standards met by males. Without awareness of the possible range of differences between the sexes, this linear approach to merit must be treated with suspicion.

The connection between nonreproductive psychological and physiological differences between the sexes and comfortable sex roles is obvious. If (as has been proved) males are more aggressive than females, then their roles ought to allow for that fact. To insist that they *not* be would involve repression. But exactly how will male roles allow aggression to be expressed? In fierce competition for success? In athletic feats? In military activity? In manipulation of powerful machines? Somewhere room should be made for its expression. Inasmuch as females will not so characteristically want to express aggression, this will amount to a difference in sex roles. Such a male role will be created by culture, to be sure, but its roots are much deeper.

Reasoning from sex differences to sex roles is, however, more complicated than this suggests. Maccoby and Jacklin explain one aspect of the problem.

It has been argued . . . that where a biological basis exists, it behooves societies to socialize children in such a way as to emphasize and exaggerate the difference. That is, since males are more aggressive, girls should be carefully trained in nonaggression throughout childhood; otherwise they will be doomed to failure and disappointment as adults in their encounters with men. . . .

The curious fact is, however, that social pressures to shape individuals toward their "natural" sex roles sometimes boomerang. Traits that may be functional for one aspect of a sex role may be dysfunctional for other aspects. A man who adopts the "machismo" image may gain prestige with his peers, or enhance his short-term attractiveness to women, at the expense of his effectiveness as a husband and father.[47]

The authors thus warn against justifying sex roles simply by reference to natural tendencies. The fabric of social relations may be upset rather than promoted by making too much of these. These authors are doubtful that fostering sex-typed behavior does serve to make for better men and women, and support the option of minimizing differences between the sexes. They conclude:

In our view, social institutions and social practices are not merely reflections of the biologically inevitable. A variety of social institutions are viable within the framework set by biology. It is up to human beings to select those that foster the life styles they most value.[48]

This sounds very simple. But how do we describe the roles that would reflect the values we hold? Is the role of a warm and nurturing father a unisex role, identical with that of a warm and nurturing mother? If equality is also one of the values to be reflected, then we would be more comfortable if both roles were really one. Difficult questions of a conceptual sort remain, as well as questions about how to *combine* values in our choice of roles, and then how to express our support of them in institutions. But it does not seem impossible.

Identifying one set of abilities with one sex is in general pernicious. If one identifies nurturing with women, for example, then for a man to nurture others is to take a feminine role. Yet we highly value male ministers and teachers and counselors, and partly they are valued because their nurturing is somewhat different from that of women. The kind of nurturing given may be sex-differentiated, then, while nurturing is not. A similar problem arises for women. Vigorous, independent, adventurous, and creative activities as well as intellectual activity are often associated with a male role; but women have the same tendencies, talents, and desires, even though they may characteristically pursue them differently. In departing from a female stereotype do they show themselves less than female? Such rigid stereotyping is unnecessary and counter productive. In this conclusion one can hardly disagree with Maccoby and Jacklin.

On the other hand, to insist that the sexes be in every dimension similar seems to me also a kind of stereotyping—androgynous stereotyping—and like the exaggerated sex-differentiated roles, these androgynous roles too may be uncomfortable and constraining. With Midgley, I am inclined to support a "piecemeal" approach to the matter of choosing roles relating the sexes, so that in the process of making new options for both sexes, our enjoyment and interest in sexual differences should not be lost, our wonder at the talents and perspective of the other sex should not be dulled. And as a guiding principle, the protection and teaching of our children and our affectionate regard for them needs to be kept in sight.

If, as the present studies suggest, the sexes are different in dimensions not connected with reproduction, we have reason for concluding that women should make their own distinctive contribution to the culture and society. Such studies suggest that representation of women's perspective is needed, and so *women* are needed in all areas of thought and art and science that affect members of both sexes.

This argument gives support to affirmative action for women. Because women are under-represented in many professions and important categories of positions, while there is no question of women's talent or intelligence, they appear to be systematically excluded. Are the procedures and tests biased? That is difficult to answer without having women in a good position to judge—so the problem is self-perpetuating. But we may suspect that there will be some difference in interpretation of tests by men and women. How can such a problem be dealt with? It is not hard to see that quotas would be not only a justifiable but perhaps the only means to correct bias or assure that there is none.

Midgley, deploring the intense competitiveness of the Western world, our obsession "with success, with examinations, tests, and record-breaking," our "behaving as if life were not worth living except at the top of the dominance hierarchy," sees one avenue of change.

> The only thing that could make the change [of women at the top of the ladder instead on only men] important would be *if* females at the top, being rather less competitive by nature than males, could do something to bring about a saner climate. To get there and do this, however, they would have to compete without catching the competitive spirit.

And she adds, "This is a lot to expect."[49] Especially if the channels to the top work effectively to weed out the women who might help make such a change.

As a support of affirmative action for women, this argument is superior to an egalitarian one. For it says that *it makes a difference* whether top positions in various areas are held exclusively by males, or by males and females both; and given that there is some relevant difference in perspective, one should prefer a mixture. If, as Justice White said, the sexes are not "fungible" and their interaction is an important "imponderable," exactly the same argument that supports their representation on juries should support their representation on important councils and major positions of influence. Women should be involved in the full spectrum of decisions that affect men and women both. This seems only reasonable and fair.

v

Our inclination to think of humans as androgynous has many roots. One that lies deep in our thinking is the idea that each human is possessed of a higher part, a rational or spiritual part, which is unaffected by sexual identity. This is the idea of an androgynous soul. It leads us toward the conclusion, also deep, that *one* figure—the figure of Everyman—can represent all of us alike. His moral struggles and education in patience and forbearance can stand for those of everyone, in every age, men and women alike. If such a representation were possible, this would signify an overwhelming similarity in our lives and perspectives and the unimportance of our differences. The question is whether it is possible.

If we were talking about another species, say chimpanzees, we would have to distinguish some of the concerns of females from those of males. The female chimpanzees spend a great part of their adult lives caring for their young. Though they bear only every five years or so and thus have widely spaced offspring, each child is the object of countless hours of play and education and watchful care. It is also for the mother to oversee the early social life of her young, to tutor the young female as the offspring learns to handle an infant, to restrain the rambunctious and reckless young males. These concerns do not enter a grown male's perspective at all. Occasionally a male will discipline or play with a young chimp, but males have no responsibility in the child-rearing process. (It is difficult to use the term "father" of the adult males here, just as it is of the worker bee—not just because there is a question of their biological parenthood, but because there is no parental *role* for them.) With these differences, what kind of figure would "Everychimp" be? Would it rove freely or would it stay with the slow and distractable young? Would it challenge for dominance or would it be content with whatever hierarchy the others find acceptable? Would it be watchful over its children or would it ignore them? The image of Everychimp can surely not ignore all such differences. If they *were* ignored, many interesting and distinctive features of its perspective would be blurred or missing. There is no androgynous chimpanzee perspective.

Or consider the langurs. For most males, life is comprised of roaming in bands, hoping for the opportunity of mating with a female, using whatever deceit may work to elude and distract the watchful, dominant male. Were a male to become dominant, it would be his role to kill unweaned infants in the female band, then to mate, and then give fatherly protection to infants born thereafter. The female's life is altogether different. Upon the birth of an infant, her attention centers about it. Should a new male take over the troop, her concern is for the safety of her infant, and she will deceive the male if it is possible, hiding it or making him think it is his. What can we say of the "Everylangur" nature? Does it incline toward the practice of infanticide? Does it protect its young from that fate? Is it free and roving or communal? One needs to allow that different patterns exist, some exhibited by males, others by females. Nor does a single individual exhibit signs of conflict between these tendencies. The "Everylangur" figure cannot contain them both; then must it leave both out? And leave out all other features relating to sex and reproduction? It appears that such a representation would have to be androgynous—but in that case it can hardly represent this two-sexed species.

Humans are no doubt less polarized than these creatures. Still if there were a single human perspective, it too should be androgynous, leaving out all reference to sex and reproduction and the care of children, leaving out the roles of mothers as well as those of fathers. But then, what will be said of the clusters of young and mature individuals—the families—which are connected with human mating. Are they too supposed to be androgynous? What unites them? From the Everyman view, one cannot say.

The idea of an androgynous soul and that of the Everyman perspective serve the egalitarian well. They reinforce the idea that we are, in all important ways, alike. The taboo against sexual identity here is logical.

VI

We have a moral commitment to the concept of a sexless human soul as the essential form of ourselves. Among its benefits is the implication that men and women are not of intrinsically different worth, that there is no difference in their moral status. But among its drawbacks is the way it deprives us of the ability to distinguish kinds of moral concerns, contrasting those that are characteristic of men with those characteristic of women. Given this state of things, either we have to seek a least common denominator to represent us—which in truth would not be a human representation at all—or we have to identify the concerns of both sexes with the concerns of one—not a propitious beginning for planning a just society. It is a conceptual dilemma.

Inasmuch as women and men have different connections to reproduction, some differences in attitude will be likely, no matter what freedom exists with respect to roles. And their moral concerns will differ some too, in emphasis if nothing else. Hear this complaint of the mother of Edward IV and Richard III, upon hearing news of Richard's latest attempt to get the throne:

> Accursed and unquiet wrangling days,
> How many of you have mine eyes beheld!
> My husband lost his life to get the crown;
> And often up and down my sons were toss'd,
> For me to joy and weep their gain and loss:
> And being seated, and domestic broils
> Clean over-blown, themselves, brother to brother, the
>   conquerors,
> Make war upon themselves;
> Blood to blood, self against self: O, preposterous
> And frantic outrage, end thy damned spleen;
> Or let me die, to look on death no more![50]

Rather than see such events, she should have strangled Richard in her womb. The anguish expressed in such terms is unequivocally a mother's.

In his most recent work, Wasserstrom makes a defense of pluralism that harmonizes well with what I have said here. He writes:

> Part of the characteristic, white, male point of view consists in the belief that reasonably well-educated, well-intentioned white males possess the capacity to view both social and natural phenomena in a detached, objective, non-distorted fashion. [Often however] the view [they hold] is one that white males hold exclusively about themselves."[51]

This fact need not seem curious. If there is an Everyman view, then there is only one right human perspective. Why should a man not think it is his? And it is not surprising that white males, as Wasserstrom says, are quite ready and eager to acknowledge that others—members of various racial groups, or women—do look at the world, approach problems, define issues, etc., through particular, nonobjective points of view. But while this is something others do, it is not something that they do.[52]

On the contrary, they are confident that "they possess the capacity and the detachment to look at things fairly, comprehensively, and completely, in short, to view things as they really are."[53] This need not be seen as sheer arrogance; it is partly the result of a conceptual framework.

The answer to such dictatorship of one perspective is the representation of others. Once we cease to stress similarities and equality, we can give some respect to pluralism, in particular to the points of view of *both* sexes. Wasserstrom adopts a pluralistic position when it comes to some institutions, such as universities. He says:

> If there are distinctive points of view that are typically connected with minority group membership, then the case for programs which make this identity relevant is in part the case for a useful and valuable type of intellectual pluralism which advances the pursuit of knowledge and the fair resolution of social issues.[54]

But the perspectives associated with women need not be represented merely in programs that are intellectual; nor is it reasonable to speak of women as constituting a "minority group membership." The pluralism that I argue for is much wider than whatever the "pursuit of knowledge" comprehends. It relates to social and moral and economic spheres as well. The pluralism I mean can be broadly stated by saying that the perspective of one sex cannot be relied on, in general, to represent the concerns of the other.

The kind of argument I have used to support women's

rights is formed along the same lines as arguments for rights of the lame or blind or retarded. Does this imply that women are, qua women, handicapped human beings? That conclusion cannot be farther from my meaning. Nevertheless women are thought of as handicapped by some thinkers, for instance Ann Ferguson:

> The two biological disadvantages of women, relative male strength and the female role in biological reproduction, explain the persistence of the sexual division of labor and the sexual stereotypes based on this.[55]

This reminds me of Mill's remark that women are weak men, and Freud's view that women can be thought of as men without a phallus. All smack of an Everyman perspective that is identifiably male. The biological features of women differentiate them; but what makes their sexual features disadvantageous is a society that does not grant respect to people with these features.

Wasserstrom speaks of "nullifying" sex differences just as we "nullify" the disadvantages of being lame or blind.[56] But this too assumes that there is a sex standard from which any deviation is a handicap or disadvantage, just as there is a set of normal capabilities with respect to seeing and hearing and moving around; the good society will treat the handicap of sex like any other, attempting to compensate for it and so to "nullify" it.

But here is a wrong order of things. Being female is a disadvantage in a society that makes it one, in particular a society which, like the Mundugumor, disparages reproduction. Do we then set out to "nullify" the injury society thus produces, as if its production were unavoidable? Why not accept a different social form? Why not put egalitarian androgynous models aside and look to a social form fitting a species of two sexes, both having their own strengths, virtues, distinctive tendencies, and weakness, neither being fully assimilable to the other? That would give a right order to our priorities.

CHAPTER SIX The Myth of Atomism

Besides the idea that human beings are made up of two parts, the one an androgynous soul, there is another reason why our thinking about justice tends to ignore distinctions of sex—our view that society is a simple collection of separate individuals. In this view, just as a gas or solid is a collection of unconnected, separate molecules, a society is a collection of individuals, each with his own basic interests and autonomy, even as he lives in association with others. I call this idea social atomism.

I

On this view or model, society is a collection of independent individual human beings who come together and make themselves into a group. Each man, on this view, *could* live without society, while, in contrast, society depends on man and is his creation. Society was created to serve some human purpose or purposes, and its existence is justified by serving them. Another way to express the view is to say that individuals are prior to society, which is derivative from their individual needs and interests. Philosophers of the seventeenth and eighteenth centuries made this picture quite clear, John Locke for instance:

> Men being ... by nature all free, equal, and independent, no one can be put out of this estate, and subjected to the political power of another, without his own consent.[1]

Because they are initially free, men's government must rest on their consent. Though government will restrict them, it does so because they are willing to be restricted, and this is to say, because it serves some purpose worth that price. This conception is echoed in many places, through many times, and sometimes takes the form of an assertion of natural rights. For those rights are sometimes called "inalienable" which man has without a political framework; and since they don't depend upon government, they cannot be abridged by government. Moreover, as men come separately into society, they are equal in doing so. The Mississippi Declaration of Rights of 1817, for instance, says that "all freemen, when they form a social compact, are equal in rights."[2] When they form a society, they come to it as free and equal. Therefore their rights within a society should be equal as well. The atomistic model is thus egalitarian and provides an argument for equal rights.

The move into society and its advantages were variously conceived. Rousseau once thought it would transform men and elevate their state:

> The transition from the state of nature to the civil state produces a very remarkable change in man, by substituting in his conduct justice for instinct and giving to his actions the morality which they previously lacked. ... Although he deprives himself in the civil state of several advantages which nature gives him, he gains such great advantages in their stead, his capacities are exercised, and developed, his

ideas are enlarged, his sentiments are ennobled, his whole soul is elevated.[3]

Others were less sanguine. Hobbes thought society was necessary simply to save man from continual warfare against his fellows. But all agreed that the benefits justified the move into a social state.

The idea is expressed in modern theories where, again, society is valued for different reasons. Like Hobbes, the modern political philosopher Robert Nozick claims that society is necessary for peaceful relations among humans: "Private and personal enforcement of one's rights," he declares, "leads to feuds, to an endless series of acts of retaliation and exactions of compensation."[4] In society there is an organization to enforce agreements and policy, to act as surrogates for an individual protecting individual rights. By contrast, philosopher John Rawls sees society as positively benefiting its members in their pursuit of individual interests. He writes:

> Since the principle for an individual is to advance as far as possible his own welfare, his own system of desires, the principle for society is to advance as far as possible the welfare of the group, to realize to the greatest extent the comprehensive system of desire arrived at from the desires of its members.[5]

The society's principle is to advance the interests of its members in a "comprehensive system of desire." And in so doing it follows principles that all the members as individuals will find fair and equitable.

The idea that a society is an association of individuals who elect to live in it is not threatened by the fact that we do not actually make such an agreement, instead passively accepting the society in which we find ourselves as children. For the myth of the contract serves a definite purpose in spite of the absence of an agreement, namely, it serves to make the power and the policies of the state depend for their legitimacy on the citizens' agreement to them.

Society is their creature and so their servant, and it has no interests entirely apart from theirs. Furthermore no one can forfeit his autonomy to the state; the moral authority of an individual is, on the contrary, the reference for judging the morality of his government.

This concept of society is often connected with the idea that individuals possess souls of identical worth. As the Christian conception of mankind is that of a collection of souls, so the social contract theory conceives of society as a collection of freemen. It is in individual persons that both moral and political authority ultimately reside.

Society is derivative. In his natural state, each man is a kind of island, and comes into society only for sound and rational reasons. Unlike other creatures who flock together from instinct—fish and deer and birds and ants—man joins with others rationally, reflectively. This choice is justified insofar as society serves the interests that led him to join it. Therefore, an individual is always in a position to criticize the policies of his government, and it in turn is accountable to him and his morality.

On this view each individual has separate interests, desires, faculties, and is by nature autonomous. Precisely these characteristics give an individual both the ability to create and the authority to criticize the state. So, as the gas in a container is formed of molecules which bounce around, competing for space and freedom to move, one can conceive of individuals in society as being in competition with one another for the maximization of their ends.

This is not the only way to look at society, though it may

seem so. Aristotle, by contrast, saw man as essentially social, needing society to fulfill his nature. To be sure, the most rudimentary social form he recognized was the family, but a man's relations to others spread much wider as the roles of master, friend, citizen, juryman, legislator, soldier, serve to unite and bind him with others. Only in a complex and civilized society could such diverse relationships come to exist, and only there, Aristotle thought, could a man be a complete human being. On this view, man needs a society and is naturally part of one. Without his community he is a lesser creature.

This conception is echoed in more recent theories deriving from studies of social animals who "instinctively" organize themselves into groups. Like wolves, primates, and ants, humans too can be seen as *essentially* social. Harlow's infant monkeys, when they were deprived of playmates and maternal care, did not develop into autonomous individualists; they did not develop fully at all. In Midgley's phrase, a human being "comes half-finished" and is "innately programmed in such a way that he needs a culture to complete him." A human may be viewed as a creature needing the company of others of its kind: "Social animals cannot live the life they are fitted for at all without their own form of society. The demand for it is as deeply inherent as the demand for one's own future safety."[6] According to this view, our social training comes early with the first infant smiles and interactions; adult responses show a child its connection with the larger human community. Without a sense of such interactions, a child would not be *able* to join a society, however many rational reasons it had for doing so.

The view of atomism is one view among others. Although it is often used uncritically as the basis and guide to social thinking, there are profound reasons for doubting that it is a good one.

II

If society were a simple collection of individuals, and their interests in it were similar, they would come to it on equal terms. Their freedom and their desires would have the same weight, and any one might complain if his interests were not given precisely the same respect given to others. But this conception cannot accommodate the composition of a human family. Are infants and young children individuals and members of society in the same sense as their parents? They surely are not free, and they may not even know their interests. Instead, *their* interests are the proper concern of their parents, are integral with the parents' overall set of interests. But how *can* one person have another person's interests on this view? It seems impossible.

Locke struggled with the question how children fit the atomic model, and gave this solution:

> Thus we are born free as we are born rational; not that we have actually the exercise of either: age, that brings one, brings with it the other, too. And thus we see how natural freedom and subjection to parents may consist together, and are both founded on the same principle. A child is free by his father's title, by his father's understanding, which is to govern him till he hath it of his own.[7]

The child is born free and rational, but *is not* free or rational until he is grown. What does this mean: What *is* the child's relation to the rest of society, a society of free and rational adults? Certainly he does not meet adults on equal terms, as a peer, any more than he does his parents. Then is the child on this view of society an anomaly? That seems to follow.

A child is not an individual in his own right. Nor do children have any choice regarding which family contains them; there is no freedom here. Nor is a child rational or capable of knowing his own interests; even less is he in a competitive position to satisfy his desires. Yet his interests have a certain priority, and this may mean that parents ought to put aside their own interests—their own personal desires—in order to give full respect to the needs of their children. But such a form of motivation has no place within the atomistic model. For one individual to determine and seek another's interests flies in the face of the idea that an individual's interests are both separable from the interests of others and ultimate. It is as if one molecule moved aside to give more room to another, which would be inexplicable.

There is also a problem in the idea that husband and wife are joined by a compact, each willing to sacrifice some freedom in return for other satisfactions. Rawls clearly sees that there is much more involved in marriage, that "sexual affinity is the most obvious example of the need of individuals both human and animal for each other," making for a particular kind of social union in which the members are vulnerable because of their strong attachments. It may lead the parties to put aside their own interests for the interests of the other. Prudence would seem to counsel against it, however, for "when we love we accept the dangers of injury and loss."[8] Still, even in a family, Rawls sees a foundation of individual choices and common agreements:

> There must be an agreed scheme of conduct in which the excellences and enjoyments of each are complementary to the good of all. Each can then take pleasure in the actions of the others as they jointly execute a plan acceptable to everyone.[9]

Clearly the individual here ceases to pursue his own interests as separate and distinct. Instead, a couple or a family finds excellences and enjoyments that are complementary to the good of all. They will come to one set of interests and one communal plan, and from the satisfaction of these each will derive pleasure. But the plan must be acceptable to everyone.

Rawls also tells us that we can think of the family as *one* person. He says that "person" may be construed as an individual or as a family or as a corporation or other group. But construing "person" thus flexibly means than the individuals in families are not entirely that—they are now being viewed as mere *parts* or components of an individual. Unmarried adults, on the other hand, count as full persons in themselves. Thus there arises the conceptual problem how some individuals count as only a part of a person while others count as wholes. What happens to individual worth here?

That a whole family should be understood as a single individual, as one of the fundamental social units, is a traditional way of reconciling atomism with the idea of an interdependent family. Locke's statement of the issue and his solution are less tactful than Rawls's:

> The husband and wife, though they have but one common concern, yet having different understandings, will unavoidably sometimes have different wills, too; it therefore being necessary that the last determination... should be placed somewhere, it naturally falls to the man's share, as the abler and stronger.[10]

Husband and wife are different individuals, with wills of their own. One would think that, in the last determination, they form a small organization which has to make decisions in its own way, for which its members are jointly responsible. But this would conflict with the atomistic model: from the point of view of society, the parties then would neither be fully individuals, nor together be one. It is simpler to say that the husband will represent them: that saves the surface features of atomism. Like a single person, the head of a family speaks for an atomic unit.

The atomistic model pushes us to one or other of two unsuitable images of families. A family is generally not simply an association of autonomous individuals, formed to further their individual ends; on the contrary, their interests are joined, intertwined, in ways that individualism cannot account for. Then do all the members make up one individual? That is incongruous. Still we honor the model, in the face of conceptual difficulties. Consider one of the problems connected with women's suffrage: if the family is an individual or speaks as one, then it should have only one vote. But whose vote should that be? That is a puzzle. Or consider a different kind of difficulty. Income tax schedules for single versus married adults pose a chronic problem partly because each member of a couple is thought of in some ways as an individual, in some ways as part of a larger whole. And more recently there have been questions about credit and financial responsibility: do these pertain to a couple as one "person" or to each individual of the couple taken separately? One can understand that there are difficulties in treating each member of the pair as a separate independent individual, each responsible for his or her debts. But there are terrible problems in treating couples as one person with only a single spokesman. The general nature of the conflict between constructions is shown in this irritable remark of Tolstoi's.

> Woman, as Christian, has a right to equality. Woman, as a member of the modern and perfectly pagan family must not struggle for an impossible equality. The modern family is like a tiny little boat sailing in a storm on a vast ocean. It can keep afloat if it is ruled by *one* will.[11]

As a Christian, each woman has a soul equal to anyone's. As a wife, she cannot count the same as her husband, the same as unmarried men and women. For then the fabric of the family would come apart—as indeed it already has, according to the writer. Having reached this conclusion, Tolstoi adds that "the man, however bad, is in the majority of cases the more sensible of the two."

It is ironic that, thanks to social atomism, a patriarchal husband-figure has been incorporated into an individualistic theory of society. Such a figure is necessary, in fact, precisely to maintain the image of a collection of individuals. Yet one virtue of such atomism is its power to *undermine* justifications for patriarchal government, this to be accomplished by insisting on the equality of human souls and human worth. It is now evident, however, that this was not a consistent program. The "impossible equality" Tolstoi refers to is the impossible reconciliation of the model of society as a collection of souls with the nonindividualistic character of human families. In the model, married women and young children are anomalies. They could be conceived as the property of the husband or as an extension of him, but not as separate individuals—which in this model means not as people at all.

This consequence is irremediable. A defender of atomism or individualism might argue that any alternative will be a theory that supports some form of natural domination by some over others, and this conclusion is anathema. But a more rational answer is that an alternative model is needed for understanding marriages and families, as well as communities of other kinds. We need a model that allows for organic connections, some more fundamental than others, among people, connections of dependency and interdependency of many kinds. They are found in various groups, among people at work, among people who join to play games, as well as in various forms of family—the families where we were children and the families where we have children of our own, and families made of both taken together, and so on. Sometimes such organizations need, or want, to speak with a single voice, and then they need a way to reconcile their separate viewpoints. Sometimes they need procedures to make action possible, bringing different proposals to a single focus. These problems can be dealt with in various ways. It hardly seems necessary for a social philosophy to decide who, in general, will be the best spokesman. Indeed, for the conclusion that a husband should "naturally" represent a couple, the argument appears to be a new form of justification of exactly the kind of power that social individualism was intended to oppose.

III

In supposing human beings to be the principal units of a society, the atomic model treats them like molecules in a chamber or marbles in a bag. It supposes them separate and similar. Rawls, for example, once described society as a group of persons who have "roughly similar needs and interests, equal in power and ability to guarantee that in normal circumstances none is able to dominate the others." Given such a group of people, he can define justice as follows:

> Justice is the virtue of practices where there are assumed to be competing interests and conflicting claims, and where it is supposed that persons will press their rights on each other. That persons are mutually self-interested in certain situations and for certain purposes is what gives rise to the question of justice in practices covering those circumstances.[12]

Justice, Rawls says in this essay, is derived from the notion of fairness, and the kind of fairness he means is that of "fair games, fair competition, and fair bargains." Fair competition among individuals with conflicting interests is at the heart of social justice.

That people are similar sets the stage for equality. In particular it encourages the idea that all may be peers, none standing in authority over another, none dependent on another. But as we have seen, such an image does not represent a human society. A society is made up of people related and connected in a variety of ways, some of which demand the sacrifice of self-interest, and some of which demand that a person's interest be identified with that of others. It is just not possible to consider them all on a par, nor therefore to view people in society as competing for their separate interests. That is one difficulty with the atomistic model. Another difficulty concerns its use of competition.

If people were alike, as two pennies or two peas, then free competition among them could be expected to have random results. What a given person loses today, he or she may win back tomorrow. The chances and power are even. There would be no advantage to one that did not also accrue to others. When Rawls specifies that no person is able to dominate the others, he builds this condition into his idea of fair competition.[13]

The model of atomism leads, then, to a concept of justice based on a competition among individual interests. Although the details of theories differ, the basic idea is that individuals have their own interests, and to get along in society they need rules which will be fair to them all as they separately pursue their desires. Such pursuit is, I believe, what is meant in the Constitution by the "pursuit of happiness."

However, the fairness of games can be of different kinds, depending on the nature of the game. A game of chance, like shooting craps, is fair if everyone has an equal chance to win. In this game, all players are equal—provided the game is fair. But in a race, only the fastest contestant should win; if he is not given the prize, the contest is unfair. So not everyone has an equal chance to win here. If one is not a good runner, there's no point in starting. It matters, then, which kind of fair game one has in mind, which kind of competition.

If people were similar, like molecules and marbles, then the competition among them would be fair if none had any advantage. The game would be managed with this in mind. And everyone who had an opportunity to play would have an equal opportunity to win. Equal opportunity then would mean an equal chance for success.

But if people are not alike, then the competition will be different. It may be a competition in which only the best should win. And in that case, although everyone has an equal opportunity to compete, the chances of winning will be concentrated among a few. Success will reflect merit, and random patterns of winners would suggest unfairness rather than fairness in the game.

If the competitions society recognizes are competitions where some have great ability while others have little or none, then regardless of how fair the game and how equal the opportunity for everyone to get in, the results will widely differentiate people. As the philosopher Thomas Nagel observed:

> The liberal idea of equal treatment demands that people receive equal opportunities if they are equally qualified by talent or education to utilize those opportunities. In requiring the relativization of equal treatment to characteristics in which people are very unequal, it guarantees that the social order will reflect and probably magnify the initial distinctions produced by nature and the past.[14]

If society rewards people for having special abilities, then "equal opportunity" to get those rewards will be meaningless except for those who have the abilities. Not only will society recognize "inequalities" with respect to these things, but it will create and foster other inequalities, in wealth for example, by rewarding some such skills or characteristics. But the justice of such a system is not self-evident . On the contrary, Nagel argues, having abilities and skills may have nothing to do with what people deserve:

> In fact, I believe that nearly all characteristics are irrelevant to what people deserve in [the way of rewards], and that most people therefore deserve to be treated equally. Perhaps voluntary differences in effort or moral differences in conduct have some bearing on economic and social desert. I do not have a precise view about what features are relevant. I contend only that they are features in which most poeple do not differ enough to justify very wide differences in reward. [15]

Whatever differences exist among people, Nagel is inclined to think they have nothing to do with what people deserve. Therefore differences do not justify greatly unequal economic and social rewards.

This view is disputed by others who see in "equal opportunity" the fair and just encouragement of those with superior abilities to excel. Vlastos, although he would limit the range of the rewards, proposes this thought-experiment: Think of a purely economic society of two individuals, A and B, A being the more efficient producer. An angel is set over them, providing for their well being. But he can only give them well being through their own efforts: "all the angel can do for them is to propose to them new practices." Should he offer them a rule that rewards them with praise according to their production?[16] Vlastos argues that such a rule would benefit both A and B, assisting them in attaining "well-being and freedom at the highest obtainable level."

In benefiting both, it must be fair. He then applies the same argument to economic rewards, and to economic and political power: differences in these as well can be justified by appeal to an equal right of everyone to benefits which can only be gotten in this way.[17]

If people are dissimilar, then free competition among them may enhance the differences they begin with, giving to the weaker and less able a more trying life and more difficult circumstances to deal with, while giving to the stronger greater resources with which to continue their successful contest of talent or skills. The result is inevitably a widening gap in rewards unless the process is controlled. But control interferes with the fairness of the competition. One justification for the differential rewards is that they come about by a competition that is fair—the freer and more open, the fairer. But what if they lead to an unjust distribution of goods? Then we have to ask the deeper ethical question, whether the results of fair competition are fair.

If the fairness of competition were all that determined fairness of a result, and if competition were perfectly free, we would accept that people get the rewards they deserve. But as Nagel observes, what people deserve has in general nothing to do with their abilities. We acknowledge many obligations to those who can't compete successfully—the ill, those with physical and mental handicaps, and also those who just fail. This shows that success does not reflect deserts. But in that case, why do we feel bound to support the system of fair competition? I believe the primary reason is our commitment to equality in the form of equal opportunity. This even appears self-evidently just. Yet, ironically, equality of opportunity to compete is a mechanism destined to produce the grossest inequalities of rewards. With that we feel moral objection. We are faced with a serious conflict in our own commitments here, as Nagel remarks:

> Liberalism has come under increasing attack in recent years, on the ground that the familiar principle of equal treatment, with its meritocratic conception of relevant differences, seems too weak to combat the inequalities dispensed by nature and the ordinary workings of the social system.[18]

Because people are different in ways affecting their ability to compete, equality of opportunity and dramatic inequalities of result go hand in hand. And when gross inequalities occur, we feel the need to provide remedial programs to compensate those who suffer from the competitive system. But in compensating those who fail, we are unfaithful to free competition and equality of opportunity, the principles began with. We weight the dice. If fair competition were fair, such provisions would be unnecessary. If fair competition is *not* fair, the remedy is not to compensate the losers but to scrap the system. It is ironic that we try to keep the system and then mitigate its inevitable results, the results which are the very evidence that the game is fair! This shows why liberalism seems "too weak" to deal with inequalities of result. The dilemma has a conceptual source.

The historian J. R. Pole views this dilemma as a conflict between two kinds of equality, to both of which Americans have a commitment.[19] But the simpler explanation is that, intuitively, we think that commitments to equality of opportunity and to the fairness of the game ought to be good foundations for social justice. Yet the ambiguity of "fair competition" and the assumptions of the atomistic model show the fallacies of this reasoning.

The atomistic model contains a number of false assumptions. It supposes that people are similar, and that society can be seen as a simple collection of them, each with his own separate interests. This group would indeed be a society of peers. But such a society is not human. There are great disparities in the talents and skills that characterize human beings; in every part of our world are the very weak and the very strong, the self-reliant and the dependent, the mature and the young. Atomism cannot take these differences into account. Neither can it represent non-peer relationships like those of parent and child, teacher and student, or any where one person takes care of the interests of another. It thus leads to the conceptual neglect of families and groups bound together by motives other than the combined self-interests of the members. It assumes that people always associate in a basically competitive way, each with his interests defined independently of the interests of others, and so assumes that society has its justification in the egoistic terms appropriate to an individual. To this one may object that we have no clear understanding of what an individual *is* apart from a human, social context. This is where we begin our growth as infants and in a sense learn to be human, instead of entering society fully formed with a complete set of private desires. Thus the fairness of the atomistic society fails utterly to represent what is fair in a human one.

IV

The atomistic view is associated with a set of moral values that are familiar: the ultimate worth of individuals and the derivation of social values from them, the responsibility of individuals for their own actions, the value of individual freedom and independence and the right to pursue one's own desires. These are the values often meant by "individualism." Equality belongs here too; for given the atomistic model, inequalities of status would have to be introduced—imposed—on a collection of beings who are from the outset similar, and therefore equal. To espouse equality is simply to confirm the features of the model.

Using this model, it is clear why women should argue for their individual rights and claim full status as individuals, with equal opportunity for the same jobs as are available to men, to demand equal pay and equal credit and equal respect. If they are married, they protest being counted as one with, and represented by, their husbands. They are individuals as much as men. They demand their place in the model.

The merits of these demands sometimes strike us as too obvious to need stating: how could anyone doubt that women as well as men are individuals? But, as we have seen, the model does not give a credible place to such a basic social form as the human family, as it also does not represent other non-peer relationships. Married women, like children, are anomalies in it. The terms in which our society is conceived, therefore, assign married women a non-place, a supporting backstage role for the "individual" and a nurturing role for those who may become individuals. The model therefore determines certain attitudes about married women; they cannot have the same place as men without undermining the validity of the model. It is not necessary to believe that the model was designed to express a derogatory attitude toward women to see that the concepts have this influence.

The demand of women to be counted as individuals is logically made, for this is the recognized path to rights in an individualistic setting. And it is a demand of great power, since to deny it is to deny that women count at all. The model will only recognize individuals. This way of reasoning, however, has severe restrictions. In the first place, it is a great distortion of the place of married women to see them as self-interested, autonomous beings competing for the satisfaction of their interests. This way of viewing them will not lead to a recognition of the real needs such women have, and their genuine claim to a number of special rights. In the second place, using an argument for equality will actually block arguments for special rights. As the model does not allow for important human differences, it favors rights that are equal. Special rights call into question the assumptions it embodies. In the third place, this kind of argument, made from a view which allows humans in society only one kind of place vis-à-vis the places of others, encourages women to adopt that place for themselves. It encourages them to take a position that is autonomous and self-interested. To take advantage of the rights available under the model, they need to adopt life patterns similar to those of males without children. For many women, this price is too high. But this means that their interests are not represented by a demand for equal rights.

By claiming their status and rights as individuals, women implicitly accept a model that cannot fully represent them, and thus they nourish the very tree they would cut down. The demand for equal rights, understood as a step toward revising concepts about women and giving them greater importance in social thinking, is an exercise in futility. In using this argument, women undertake to conform to what the model dictates. They are in an unfortunate bind.

v

What is needed is another model, more complicated but also more useful to our deliberations about justice. We need a model that acknowledges many kinds of relations among people, and many kinds of social roles, and other kinds of interest than self-interest. In that model, what is fair will not derive from a sense in which games are fair but will appear fundamental to the game conception. In that model, competition will be only one of the relations among people where determinations of justice apply.

How will women fit in this better model? They will fit in a variety of ways and roles, depending on what real roles and functions need to be represented. Many forms of life will appear there: the career woman, married and unmarried; the wife and mother who does not want a career; the woman who wants both career and family simultaneously, without wanting two full-time jobs; the woman who seeks a career after her children are grown; the divorced woman who must combine the responsibilities of both parents. Of women who want both careers and families, Midgley's characterization of human ambivalence is apt: they want the security and warmth of the hearth and the challenge of a career in the outer world. Such a desire may be difficult to satisfy, but it is not illogical or inconsistent—not when viewed apart from atomism.

The rights needed by women in different life forms will differ. The wife and homemaker will need some special provisions for her old age; the career woman will not need these, but will need equal rights with respect to work. The woman who pursues a part-time career will need both kinds of rights less urgently; the woman whose career begins late will have a special set of needs again; while the divorced mother's needs are probably the greatest of all. The difficult problem is to formulate a program that takes cognizance of all these needs within the framework of some reasonable social cost. To acknowledge only the claims of one group and to pursue only that set of rights is just another Procrustean bed.

To acknowledge the legitimacy of these different life forms requires a different vision of society. And though it is not recognized, this may be the most important mission of the movement for women's rights. For since their demands cannot fit into the framework ready at hand, it is up to them to help create a new one. Nor does it make sense for women to refuse this responsibility, since without their participation, the old problem of perspectives is introduced again. The perspectives of both sexes need representing, not just in the political arena, but in the very conception of what society is. It is an appropriate challenge for women of spirit and imagination.

I have spoken throughout as if rights can, and often do, derive from needs. But of course not just any need will justify a right. The particular needs that I mention are not trivial or negligible; the needs of the blind and the disabled may be counted a plausible basis for special rights, though costs and competing needs may restrict them. But the question may arise, why should the needs of women—who are not disabled or weak or ill—count as justifying rights for them? The answer to that does not seem to me difficult. It involves reference to a fact that individualism obscures, that one of society's chief and rudimentary concerns is that the children in it, and the families who care for the children, and the mothers who are their primary parents, have the best support it can provide.

Notes

Introduction

1. Midgley, *Beast and Man* (Ithaca: Cornell University Press, 1978), 330n.

CHAPTER ONE Equality of the Sexes

1. John Locke, *Second Treatise on Civil Government*, Bk. I, ch. ii, para. 4. Locke added "unless the Lord and Master of them all should... set one above another, and confer on him... right to dominion and sovereignty." Americans in framing the Constitution used only the first part of Locke's principle.

2. Henry Alonzo Myers, *Are Men Equal?* (Ithaca: Cornell University Press, 1945), 136. The connection between human equality and equality of rights in American political thought is carefully traced by J. R. Pole in *The Pursuit of Equality in American History* (Berkeley: University of California Press, 1978); see ch. 6 in particular.

3. J. S. Mill and Harriet Taylor Mill, *Essays on Sex Equality* (Chicago: University of Chicago Press, 1970), 73-74.

4. *Ibid.*, 74-75.

5. *The Subjection of Women* (Cambridge, Mass.: M.I.T. Press, 1970), 48.

6. *Ibid.*, 40.

7. *Ibid.*, 59-63.

8. *Ibid.*, 4.

9. Wasserstrom, "Racism, Sexism and Preferential Treatment: An

Approach to the Topics," *U.C.L.A. Law Review,* 24 (July 1977), 586.

10. *Ibid.,* 609–610.

11. *Ibid.,* 611.

12. *Ibid.,* 611–612.

13. *Ibid.,* 610.

14. *Ibid.,* 611.

15. Jagger, "On Sexual Equality," *Ethics,* 84 (1974) 276. Although Wasserstrom says this comes "fairly close to the assimilationist view" (605–606), he also gives us grounds for objecting to it.

16. Wasserstrom, 606.

17. *Ibid.,* 615.

18. *Ibid.,* 615–616.

19. Midgley, 326.

20. New York: Harper, 1976.

21. "Nullifying sex differences" is used in Wasserstrom's book, *Philosophy and Social Issues: Five Studies* (Notre Dame: University of Notre Dame Press, 1980).

22. *Nichomachean Ethics,* Bk. V, Richard McKeon, trans. (New York: Random House, 1941), 1131aff.

23. Bedau, "Egalitarianism and the Idea of Equality," included in J. R. Pennock and J. W. Chapman, eds., *Nomos IX: Equality* (New York: Atherton Press, 1967), 13.

24. *Equality* (Cambridge, Eng.: Cambridge University Press, 1949), 5.

25. Vlastos, "Justice and Equality," included in Richard Brandt, ed., *Social Justice* (Englewood Cliffs, N.J.: Prentice-Hall, 1962), 33–34.

26. Bedau, 13.

27. Berlin, "Equality," Proceedings of the Aristotelian Society, 56 (1955–56), 315.

28. Address at Springfield, Ill., July 17, 1858, in Paul Angle, ed., *Created Equal? The Complete Lincoln-Douglas Debates of 1858* (Chicago: University of Chicago Press, 1958), 82.

29. Wasserstrom, 607.

CHAPTER TWO   Things Being Equal

1. Berlin, 301.

2. Pole, ch. 6.

3. Hart, "Are There Natural Rights?" *Philosophical Review,* 64 (April 1955).

4. Berlin, 315, 311.

5. In *Welcome to the Monkey House* (New York: Dell, 1968).

6. Bedau, 23.

7. *Republic* VIII, Steph. 557 ff.

8. Vlastos, 39–40.

9. The quoted phrases are those of William Frankena and Vlastos.

10. Vlastos, 43.

11. See Pole, 161–176, for the connection between this issue and the right of Negroes to vote.

12. Title IX of the Civil Rights Act forbids discrimination by sex in matters of employment. For some details see below, Chapter 4.

13. Dworkin, "Why Bakke Has No Case," *New York Review of Books*, Nov. 10, 1977.

14. Regents of the University of California v. Bakke, 98 S.Ct. 2733 (1978).

15. This view of moral practices and their justification draws on the conceptions of Peter Winch in *Ethics and Action* (London: Routledge and Kegan Paul, 1972) and those of D. Z. Phillips and H. O. Mounce in *Moral Practices* (New York: Schocken Books, 1970).

16. I refer the reader to Ronald Dworkin's essay "Hard Cases," for an illuminating discussion of how the reconciling of rules really works, in *Taking Rights Seriously* (Cambridge, Mass.: Harvard University Press, 1977), 81–130.

CHAPTER THREE   Peers

1. The line occurs in a CBS television production (aired January 29, 1979, KPIX, San Francisco) that featured Katharine Hepburn. Although the line does not occur in Emlyn Williams' play, the shift in relationship is marked there as well.

2. *Nichomachean Ethics*, Bk. VIII, ch. 9, 1159b.

3. *Ibid.*, ch. 4, 1157b.

4. *Ibid.*, ch. 7, 1158b.

5. Aristotle places women's souls at a lower level than men's, though higher than slaves', which are in turn superior to animals. In this way he gives content to the "inequality" of humans.

6. *Natural Rights*, 248.

7. New York: Capricorn Books, 1959. This subject is discussed further in Chapter 6, below.

8. *The Social Contract*, Charles Frankel, trans. (New York: Hafner 1947), Bk. I, ch. 9, 22. This is Rousseau's earlier view. Later he did not see the effects of society to be so salutary.

9. Wilson, *On Human Nature* (Cambridge, Mass.: Harvard University Press, 1978), 215.

10. Ardrey, *The Social Contract* (New York: Delta Books, 1970), 3.

11. Goodall, *In the Shadow of Man*, 122 ff.

12. Goodall, "Life and Death at Gombe," *National Geographic Magazine*, 155 (May 1979), 592–621, 615–616.

13. Midgley, 337.

CHAPTER FOUR Gender and the Law

1. Reed v. Reed, 404 U.S. 71 (1971).

2. Leo Kanowitz, *Sex Roles in Law and Society: Cases and Materials* (Albuquerque: University of New Mexico Press, 1973), 516–517.

3. Kanowitz, 516.

4. Quoted in Gerald Gunther, *Cases and Materials on Constitutional Law*, 9th ed. (Mineola, N.Y.: Foundation Press, 1975), 770.

5. Senate Subcommittee Hearings on the Constitutional Amendment, 91st Congress, *Women and the "Equal Rights Amendment,"* Catharine Stimpson, ed., in conjunction with the Congressional Information Service, Washington, D.C. (New York: Bowker, 1972), 12–14.

6. *Ibid.*, 14.

7. Goesaert v. Cleary, 335 U.S. 464 (1948).

8. Quoted in Gunther, 772.

9. Quoted in Gunther, 768.

10. *Ibid.*, 769.

11. Phillips v. Martin Marietta Corp., 400 U.S. 542 (1971).

12. Quoted in Gunther, 787.

13. *Ibid.*

14. *Ibid.*

15. Diaz v. Pan American World Airways, Inc., 404 U.S. 950, 92 S.Ct. 275 (1971).

16. Quoted in Kanowitz, 351.

17. *Ibid.*

18. *Ibid.*

19. *Ibid.*

20. Taylor v. Louisiana, 419 U.S. 522 (1975).

21. Quoted in Gunther, 773.

22. *Ibid.*

23. *Ibid.*, 774.

24. 417 U.S. 484 (1974).

25. Quoted in Gunther, 781.

26. *Ibid.*

27. Gunther, 781.

28. 416 U.S. 351 (1974).

29. Gunther, 783.

30. *Ibid.*
31. *Ibid.*
32. Senate Hearings on the E.R.A., 26.
33. *Ibid.*
34. *Ibid.*, 47.
35. *Ibid.*, 41.
36. *Ibid.*, 27.
37. *Ibid.*, 48.
38. *Ibid.*, 48.
39. 435 U.S. 702 (1978).
40. Gerald Gunther, ed., *Constitutional Law* (9th ed.) *and Individual Rights in Consitutional Law* (2nd ed.) *1978 Supplement: Cases and Materials* (Mineola, N.Y.: Foundation Press, 1978), 212.
41. *Ibid.*
42. *Ibid.*, 212, 213.
43. *Ibid.*, 213.
44. Phillips and Mounce, *Moral Practices* (New York: Schocken, 1970), especially chs. 2 and 5.
45. Sylvia Porter's column "Sex and Social Security" (*San Francisco Chronicle*, April 2, 1979, 55) shows how complicated is the problem of equitable social security for men and women, not just legally and economically but also conceptually. Our present social concepts are incapable of representing sex-differentiated issues coherently. The following chapter attempts to explore some of the reasons for this.
46. Dworkin, "Why Bakke Has No Case," 12.
47. Senate Hearings on E.R.A., 21.
48. *Ibid.*, 30.
49. *Ibid.*, 28.

CHAPTER FIVE   A Two-sexed Species

1. *The Marble Faun: or the Romance of Monte Beni*, The Centenary Edition (Columbus, Ohio: Ohio State University Press, 1968), Vol. IV, 39-40.
2. Weininger, *Sex and Character*, authorized trans. (London: Heineman; New York: Putnam, 1906), 65.
3. *Ibid.*, 68.
4. *Ibid.*, 71.
5. *Ibid.*, 190.
6. *Ibid.*, 346.
7. *Ibid.*, 348.

8. Mead, *Male and Female* (New York: Morrow, 1975), chs. 3–7.

9. *Ibid.*, 98, 99.

10. *Ibid.*, 100.

11. *Ibid.*, 368–369.

12. Midgley, 326.

13. Midgley provides an interesting discussion of how we employ a conception of animals and animal nature to characterize our own morality, ch. 2.

14. This account derives from Sarah Blaffer Hrdy's *The Langurs of Abu* (Cambridge, Mass.: Harvard University Press, 1977).

15. This account is drawn from Jane Goodall's *In the Shadow of Man.*

16. This account is taken from C. R. Carpenter, "A Field Study in Siam of the Behavior and Social Relations of the Gibbon," included in *Primate Social Behavior*, Charles H. Southwick, ed. (Princeton: Van Nostrand, 1963).

17. Lorenz, *On Aggression*, Marjorie Kerr Wilson, trans. (New York: Harcourt Brace, 1966), 203; cited by Midgley, 349.

18. Richard Fiennes, *The Order of Wolves* (Indianapolis: Bobbs-Merrill, 1976).

19. Mead, 189.

20. *Ibid.*, 194.

21. Eibl-Eibesfeldt, *Love and Hate* (New York: Schocken Books, 1974), 156.

22. Mead, 202.

23. *Ibid.*, 205.

24. Goodall, 193.

25. *Ibid.*

26. *Ibid.*, 191–192.

27. Midgley, 282.

28. *Ibid.*, 302.

29. *Ibid.*

30. *Ibid.*, 304.

31. *Ibid.*, 40.

32. *Ibid.*, 41.

33. Harry F. Harlow, "Love in Infant Monkeys," *Scientific American*, 204 (June 1959).

34. Jane English, an introductory essay on sex roles and gender in Mary Vetterling-Braggin, Frederick Ellston, and Jane English, eds., *Feminism and Philosophy* (Totowa, N.Y.: Littlefield, Adams, 1977), 39.

35. Ferguson, "Androgyny as an Ideal for Human Development," in *Feminism and Philosophy*, 45.

36. *Ibid.*, 61.

37. This point is the thesis of Dorothy Dinnerstein's *The Mermaid and the Minotaur: Sexual Arrangements and the Human Malaise* (New York: Harper, 1976), though she argues the issue from the point of androgyny in parenthood rather than in terms of flexible parent roles.

38. Midgley, 300.

39. *Ibid.*, 298.

40. Mead, 368.

41. Midgley, 329.

42. English, *Feminism and Philosophy*, 40–41.

43. J. M. Bardwick, *Psychology of Women* (New York: Harper & Row, 1971), 102.

44. Eleanor E. Maccoby, ed., *The Development of Sex Differences* (Stanford: Stanford University Press, 1966), 25–55.

45. Debora P. Waber, "Sex Differences in Mental Abilities, Hemispheric Lateralization, and Rate of Physical Growth at Adolescence," *Developmental Psychology*, 13 (1977), 29–38; also D. P. Waber, "Sex Differences in Cognition: A Function of Maturation Rate?" *Science*, 192 (May 7, 1976), 572–573.

46. Maccoby and Jacklin, *The Psychology of Sex Differences* (Stanford: Stanford University Press, 1974), 349–355, 360–363.

47. Maccoby and Jacklin, 373–374.

48. *Ibid.*, 374.

49. Midgley, 330.

50. William Shakespeare, *King Richard III*, Act II, sc. iv.

51. Wasserstrom, *Philosophy and Social Issues: Five Studies* (Notre Dame, Ind.: University of Notre Dame Press, 1980), 57–58.

52. *Ibid.*, 58.

53. *Ibid.*

54. *Ibid.*, 59–60.

55. Ferguson, 52.

56. Wasserstrom, *Philosophy and Social Issues*, 36ff.

CHAPTER SIX   The Myth of Atomism

1. Locke, *Second Treatise on Civil Government*, par. 95.

2. Quoted in Ritchie, 245.

3. *The Social Contract*, I, ch. 8. I use Ritchie's translation here.

4. Nozick, *Anarchy, State and Utopia* (New York: Basic Books, 1968), 11.

5. Rawls, *A Theory of Justice* (Cambridge, Mass.: Harvard University Press, 1971), 23-24.

6. Midgley, 286, 300.

7. *Second Treatise*, ch. 6, par. 61.

8. Rawls, 525, 573.

9. *Ibid.*, 526.

10. *Second Treatise*, ch. 7, par. 82.

11. A. B. Goldenveizer, *Talks with Tolstoi*, S. S. Koteliansky and Virginia Woolf, trans. (Richmond, Eng.: Hogarth Press, 1923), 28-29.

12. Rawls, "Justice as Fairness," *Philosophical Review*, 67 (April 1958), 171, 175, 178.

13. I am here in large agreement with Thomas Nagel, that Rawls's "original position" is an egalitarian one (*Philosophical Review*, 82 [April 1973], 220). This is only the roughest sketch of Rawl's position; his end view is subtle and complicated, and cannot be adequately represented here. I deal primarily with his assumptions and the "original position" that expresses them.

14. Nagel, "Equal Treatment and Compensatory Discrimination," *Philosophy and Public Affairs*, 2 (Summer 1973), 348-363; reprinted in Tom L. Beauchamp, ed., *Ethics and Public Policy* (Englewood Cliffs, N.J.: Prentice-Hall, 1975), 48.

15. *Ibid.*

16. Vlastos, 66-67.

17. *Ibid.*, 70, 71.

18. Nagel, "Equal Treatment," 353.

19. Pole, particularly ch. 11.

Bibliography

Ardener, Edwin. "Belief and the Problem of Women." In Shirley Ardener, ed., *Perceiving Women*.

Ardener, Shirley, ed. *Perceiving Women*. New York: John Wiley, 1975.

Ardrey, Robert. *The Social Contract*. New York: Delta Books, 1970.

Aristotle. *The Basic Works of Aristotle*. Richard McKeon, ed., New York: Random House, 1941.

Bedau, Hugo Adam. "Egalitarianism and the Idea of Equality." In J. R. Pennock and J. W. Chapman, eds., *Nomos IX: Equality*.

Brandt, Richard B., ed. *Social Justice*. Englewood Cliffs, N.J.: Prentice-Hall, 1962.

Brown, William. *An Essay on the Natural Equality of Men*, 2d ed. London: Dilly and Cadell, 1794.

Carpenter, C. R. "A Field Study in Siam of the Behavior and Social Relations of the Gibbon." In Charles H. Southwick, ed., *Primate Social Behavior*.

Chodorow, Nancy. "Family Structure and Feminine Personality." In Michelle Rosaldo and Louise Lamphere, eds., *Woman, Culture and Society*.

———. *The Reproduction of Mothering*, Berkeley and Los Angeles: University of California Press, 1978.

Dinnerstein, Dorothy, *The Mermaid and the Minotaur: Sexual Arrangements and the Human Malaise*, New York: Harper, 1976.

Dworkin, Ronald, *Taking Rights Seriously*, Cambridge, Mass.: Harvard University Press, 1977.

———. "Why Bakke Has No Case." *New York Review of Books*, Nov. 10, 1977, 11–15.

Eibl-Eibesfeldt, Irenäus. *Love and Hate*. New York: Schocken Books, 1974.

English, Jane, ed. *Sex Equality*. Englewood Cliffs, N.J.: Prentice-Hall, 1977.

———. "Sex Roles and Gender." In Mary Vetterling-Braggin, Frederick A. Elliston, and Jane English, eds., *Feminism and Philosophy*.

Feinberg, Joel. "Noncomparative Justice." *Philosophical Review*, 83 (July 1974), 297–338.

Fiennes, Richard. *The Order of Wolves*. Indianapolis: Bobbs-Merrill, 1976.

Fiss, Own M. "Groups and the Equal Protection Clause." *Philosophy and Public Affairs* 5 (Winter 1976), 107–177.

Friederich, Carl J., and John W. Chapman, eds. *Nomos VI: Justice*. New York: Atherton Press, 1963.

Golding, William. *Lord of the Flies*. New York: Capricorn Books, 1959.

Goodall, Jane van Lawick. *In the Shadow of Man*. New York: Dell Books, 1971.

———. "Life and Death at Gombe." *National Geographic Magazine*, 155 (May 1979), 592–621.

Gunther, Gerald. *Cases and Materials on Constitutional Law*, 9th ed. Mineola, N.Y.: Foundation Press, 1975.

———. *Constitutional Law* (9th ed.) *and Individual Rights in Constitutional Law* (2d ed.), *1978 Supplement: Cases and Materials*. Mineola, N.Y.: Foundation Press, 1978.

Haggard, Henry Rider. *She, a History of Adventure*. London: Macdonald, 1963.

Hare, R. M. *Freedom and Reason*. New York: Oxford University Press, 1965.

Harlan, Louis R. *Separate and Unequal*. New York: Atheneum, 1968.

Harlow, Harry F. "Love in Infant Monkeys." *Scientific American*, 200 (June 1959), 68–74.

———, and Harlow, M. K. "Social Deprivation in Monkeys." *Scientific American*, 207 (Nov. 1963), 136–146.

Hart, H. L. A. "Are There Any Natural Rights?" *Philosophical Review*, 64 (April 1955), 175–191.

Hawthorne, Nathaniel. *The Marble Faun: or The Romance of Monte Beni*,

The Centenary Edition, Vol. IV. Columbus, O.: Ohio State University Press, 1968.

Hrdy, Sarah Blaffer, *The Langurs of Abu*. Cambridge, Mass.: Harvard University Press, 1977.

Jaggar, Alison. "On Sexual Equality." *Ethics*, 84 (1974), 275-291.

——. "Political Philosophies of Women's Liberation." In Mary Vetterling-Braggin, Frederick A. Elliston, and Jane English, eds., *Feminism and Philosophy*.

Jung, Emma, *Animus and Anima*. Cary G. Baynes and Hildegard Nagel, trans. Zurich: Spring Publishing, 1972.

Kanowitz, Leo. *Sex Roles in Law and Society: Cases and Materials*. Albuquerque, N.M.: University of New Mexico Press, 19 73.

——. *Women and the Law: The Unfinished Revolution*. Albuquerque, N.M.: University of New Mexico Press 1969.

Lafitte, Paul. *Le Paradoxe de l'Egalité*. Paris: Librairie Hatchette, 1887.

Lakoff, Robin, *Language and Women's Place*. New York: Harper & Row, 1975.

Lakoff, Sanford A. *Equality in Political Philosophy*. Cambridge, Mass.: Harvard University Press, 1964.

Landsdell, H. "Sex Differences in Hemispheric Asymmetries of the Human Brain." *Nature*, 203 (1964), 550.

Laslett, Peter, and W. G. Runciman. *Philosophy, Politics and Society*. Oxford: Blackwell, 1969.

Leis, Nancy B. "Women in Groups: Ijaw Women's Associations." In Michelle Rosaldo and Louise Lamphere, eds., *Women, Culture and Society*.

Locke, John. *Two Treatises of Government*. New York and London: Harper, 1966.

Maccoby, Eleanor. *The Development of Sex Differences*. Stanford: Stanford University Press, 1966.

——, and C. N. Jacklin. *The Psychology of Sex Differences*. Stanford: Stanford University Press, 1974.

Mahowald, Mary Briody. *Philosophy of Woman: Classical to Current Concepts*. Indianapolis: Hacket Publishing, 1978.

Mead, Margaret. *Male and Female*. New York: Morrow, 1975.

Midgley, Mary. *Beast and Man: The Roots of Human Nature*. Ithaca, N.Y.: Cornell University Press, 1978.

Mill, John Stuart. *The Subjection of Women*. Cambridge, Mass.: Harvard University Press, 1970.

——, and Harriet Taylor Mill. *Essays on Sex Equality*. Alice S. Rossi, ed. Chicago: University of Chicago Press, 1970.

Myers, Henry Alonzo. *Are Men Equal?* Ithaca, N.Y.: Cornell University Press, 1945.

Nagel, Thomas. "Rawls on Justice." *Philosophical Review*, 82 (April 1973), 220.

———. "Equal Treatment and Compensatory Discrimination." In Tom Beauchamp, ed., *Ethics and Public Policy*. Englewood Cliffs, N.J.: Prentice-Hall, 1975.

Nozick, Robert. *Anarchy, State and Utopia*. New York: Basic Books, 1968.

Pennock, J. Roland, and John W. Chapman, eds. *Nomos IX: Equality*. New York: Atherton Press, 1967.

Phillips, D. Z., and H. O. Mounce. *Moral Practices*. New York: Schocken Books, 1970.

Plato. *The Republic*. Francis M. Cornford, trans. New York: Oxford University Press, 1945.

Poirier, Frank E. *Primate Socialization*. New York: Random House, 1972.

Pole, J. R. *The Pursuit of Equality in American History*. Berkeley and Los Angeles: University of California Press, 1978.

Porter, Sylvia. "Sex and Social Security." *San Francisco Chronicle*, April 2, 1979.

Rawls, John. "Justice as Fairness." *Philosophical Review*, 67 (April 1958), 164.

———. *A Theory of Justice*. Cambridge, Mass.: Harvard University Press, 1971.

Ritchie, David. *Natural Rights*. London: Allen and Unwin, 1952.

Rosaldo, Michelle, and Louise Lamphere, eds. *Woman, Culture and Society*. Stanford: Stanford University Press, 1974.

Rousseau, Jean-Jacques. "The Social Contract." In *The Political Writings of Jean-Jacques Rousseau*. C. E. Vaughan, trans. Cambridge, Eng.: Cambridge University Press, 1915.

Southwick, Charles H., ed. *Primate Social Behavior*. Princeton: Van Nostrand, 1963.

Tanner, Nancy. "Matrifocality in Indonesia and Africa and among Black Americans." In Michelle Rosaldo and Louise Lamphere, eds., *Woman, Culture and Society*.

Thomson, David. *Equality*. Cambridge, Eng.: Cambridge University Press, 1949.

Tinbergen, Niko. *The Animal and Its World*. Cambridge, Mass.: Harvard University Press, 1972.

Tolstoi, Leo. "The Kreuzer Sonata." *The Works of Tolstoi*, Vol. XVI. New York: Scribners, 1899.

———, and A. B. Goldenveizer. *Talks with Tolstoi*. S. S. Koteliansky and Virginia Woolf, trans. Richmond, Eng.: Hogarth Press, 1923.

Turnbull, Colin. *The Mountain People*. New York: Simon and Schuster, 1972.

United States Senate, Subcommittee Hearings on the Equal Rights Amendment. *Women and the "Equal Rights Amendment."* Catherine Stimson, ed. New York and London: Bowker, 1972.

Vetterling-Braggin, Mary, Frederick A. Elliston, and Jane English, eds. *Feminism and Philosophy*. Totowa, N.J.: Littlefield Adams, 1977.

Vlastos, Gregory. "Justice and Equality." In R. Brandt, ed., *Social Justice*.

Vonnegut, Kurt. "Harrison Bergeron." Reprinted in *Welcome to the Monkey House*. New York: Dell Publishing, 1968.

Waber, D. P. "Sex Differences in Cognition: A Function of Maturational Rate?" *Science*, 192 (1976), 572–573.

———. "Sex Difference in Mental Abilities, Hemispheric Lateralization, and Rate of Physical Growth at Adolescence." *Developmental Psychology*, 13 (Jan. 1977), 29–38.

Wasserstrom, Richard. *Philosophy and Social Issues: Five Studies*. Notre Dame: University of Notre Dame Press, 1980.

———. "Racism, Sexism and Preferential Treatment: An Approach to the Topics." *U.C.L.A. Law Review*, July 1977, 581–622.

Weininger, Otto. *Sex and Character*. London and New York: Putnam, 1906.

Wilson, Edward O. *On Human Nature*. Cambridge, Mass.: Harvard University Press, 1978.

———. *Sociobiology*. Cambridge, Mass.: Harvard University Press, 1975.

Winch, Peter. *Ethics and Action*. London: Routledge & Kegan Paul, 1972.

Wittig, M. A., and A. C. Petersen, eds. *Sex Related Differences in Cognitive Functioning*, New York: Academic Press, 1979.

Index

SUBJECT

Index

NAMES

Index

Library of Congress Cataloging in Publication Data

Wolgast, Elizabeth Hankins, 1929-
    Equality and the rights of women.

    Bibliography: p. 167.
    Includes index.
    1. Women's rights—United States. 2. Equality. 3. Women—Legal status, laws,
etc.—United States. I. Title.
HQ1426.W58   301.41′2′0973   79-24710
ISBN 0-8014-1211-0